The Human Face
of God

To: My loving husband,

Fr. David R. Cruz

Blessings!

The Human Face of God

"A Collection of Stories and Biblical Reflections on the Spiritual Life"

David R. Cruz

Pleasant Word (a division of WinePress Publishing, PO Box 428, Enumclaw, WA 98022) functions only as book publisher. As such, the ultimate design, content, editorial accuracy, and views expressed or implied in this work are those of the author.

Unless otherwise noted, all Scriptures are taken from the translation of the Bible, The Good News Translation, Catholic Edition published by the American Bible Society.

ISBN 13: 978-1-4141-0711-0
ISBN 10:1-4141-0711-0
Library of Congress Catalog Card Number: 2006901377

Table of Contents

Introduction   vii

Chapter I: Trust Has a Face   11
Chapter II: Mercy Has a Face   23
Chapter III: Compassion Has a Face   37
Chapter IV: Forgiveness Has a Face   51
Chapter V: Courage Has a Face   69
Chapter VI: Hope Has a Face   83
Chapter VII: The Bridge Builder Has a Face   97

Endnotes   115
Appendix of Prayers   119
Acknowledgements   133
About the Author   135

Introduction

The introduction of a book is intended to be like a road map. It gives the reader guidance and direction to travel more easily from chapter to chapter. Much like a road map facilitates the journey so that one can reach their final destination without getting off course, I hope this introduction will provide a clear point of departure for the reader.

My purpose for writing this book is not to add one more book to the list of religious books. Indeed, for me, books that are labeled "religious" oftentimes tend to be sectarian or exclusive. Instead, I hope this book will encourage a broader way of looking at, and relating to God. Although, as a Catholic, I may see things from a Catholic perspective, I have made every attempt to be inclusive of other spiritual points of view. To this end, I have incorporated the insights of authors from a variety of Christian and Jewish traditions. I have often found that their perspectives enrich my own spiritual life, and I hope that their insights will enrich the reader as well.

When I explored a possible symbol or metaphor that could hold this narrative together, I continually found myself returning to the image of the face. As the chapters begin to unfold, the reader will notice the use of the image as it appears in the Scriptures and other spiritual works. I marvel as I am continuously reminded of the image as it occurs in the ordinary moments of daily life.

Consider in your own human experience the power of the symbol of the face. Whether it is the dignified face of Lincoln sculpted on Mt. Rushmore, the face the Old Man of the Mountain, carved by the passage of time on the granite cliffs of New Hampshire, the grotesque bloodied face of the crucified Christ on the cover of Time, or the photograph of the lovely face of a deceased parent or spouse taken during happy times, the image of the human face always seems to evoke a powerful emotional response.

Perhaps that is why the writers of the Hebrew Scriptures employ the symbol of the face to express certain attributes and characteristics of God's personality. For instance, Jeremiah, the prophet, records God's disapproval when he writes, "For I have set my face against the city." To express God's favor and blessing, the author of the book of Numbers writes, "The Lord let his face shine upon you. The Lord look upon you kindly and give you peace." Similarly, God speaks through the Prophet Ezekiel saying, "No longer will I hide my face from them, for I have poured out my spirit upon the house of Israel." And, the psalmist invokes God's divine favor by uttering the words, "Lord of hosts restore us; let your face shine upon us, that we may be saved."

While the Old Testament records these or similar words about the face of God, ironically, not much is said in the New Testament about the face of Jesus. References about the face of Jesus are virtually non-existent, and nowhere to be found is a detailed description of Jesus' physical appearance. That such a basic description is missing from the earliest accounts of the life of the earthly Jesus is perhaps by coincidence or by design. Nevertheless, no physical description of Jesus was ever given to us by those who knew him and saw his face.

As a result, the following pages are an invitation to the reader to rediscover and recognize the face of Jesus, as he continues to reveal himself in the faces of the young, the old, the poor the affluent, the wounded, the wise, the neglected, the contented, the abused, the hopeful, the courageous, the despised, the fearful, the sick, the healthy, and the ordinary. It is in these ordinary faces that he is continually trying to reveal himself to us and to the world. And, just as we can unexpectedly recognize a familiar face in a crowd, it can be said of the human face of God that while it is often partially hidden and obscured, it is also waiting to be recognized and rediscovered in the faces of ordinary people and ordinary moments.

I hope that this collection of personal stories, prayers, poems and spiritual writings will assist the reader to begin to search for the face of Jesus in the ordinary moments, events, and struggles of daily life. In time I hope that we can all begin to understand, at least in part, that trust, mercy, compassion, forgiveness, courage and hope, all have a human face. And by the end of the final chapter the reader will realize that we are all invited to become human faces of God in our own lives and in the lives of others.

With this, the "road map" portion of this narrative comes to a close. Without further delay, I invite the reader to begin a journey of rediscovering the human face of God. I pray that as you travel along your own particular road that God will let his face shine upon you, be gracious unto you, and give you mercy, courage and peace.

Chapter I

Trust Has a Face

⤳⁂☊

It was just after daybreak, as the sun began to rise over the horizon, when they observed him from their boat. Standing next to a charcoal fire, with fish and bread on it, he waited on the shore of Galilee. In a voice unmistakably his, he said, ""Bring some of the fish you have just caught. Come and eat." After they had eaten, Jesus said to Simon Peter, "Simon son of John, do you love me more than these others do?" "Yes, Lord. You know that I love you." Peter answered three times. Ironically, it had also been next to a charcoal fire in a courtyard, that Peter had denied knowing him three times. And then Jesus said to the fisherman, "I am telling you the truth: when you were young, you used to get ready and go anywhere you wanted to; but when you are old, you will stretch out your hands and someone else will tie you up and take you where you don't want to go."[1]

A KNOCK AT MIDNIGHT

Shortly after midnight on July 28, 1981, three members of a Guatemalan death squad knocked on the door of a little village rectory where Fr. Stan Rother, the village priest, lay sleeping. Roused from his sleep, Fr. Stan had feared that such a knock would come in the middle of the night. He had been back at his post in the village of Santiago de Atitlan since the spring of the same year, when he had been warned by his family, back in Oklahoma, not to go back to the village. But how could, he not return, he thought. Who would shepherd his flock? With so much civil unrest in the countryside, who would care for the needs of the people?

In loud, threatening voices, Stan was ordered to go with them immediately. Fearing that he would be tortured, Stan resisted, struggled, and fought with all his strength. It was three against one, but surely he could overpower his would-be abductors. After all, as a young man, he had been a farmer and was the son of Oklahoma farmers. Now, 46, his body, lean and muscular, had been tempered and weather-beaten by the hard work of the Guatemalan countryside. But, alas, with all his might, he could not overpower the strength of three men with their weapons of death. Like a loud cry of a wounded sparrow his words echoed into the moonlit night, "No, I won't go with you! You'll have to kill me here!"[2] Suddenly the terrifying sounds of gunshots filled the village sky, and Fr. Stan lay still.

The following morning the people of Santiago de Atitlan and the surrounding villages felt a mixture of outrage and sorrow at the news of the murder of their parish priest. "Padre Aplas" as Fr. Stan was known by the people, had been their friend and companion for the past thirteen years. Since his arrival in 1968, Stan had learned their native language, visited their humble homes, taught them to plant new crops for their families, and built their local clinic. In their eyes, "Padre Aplas" had become repairman, carpenter, chauffeur, farmer, counselor, and friend. Most of all, he had been their spiritual guide. He had presided at their baptisms, weddings, funerals and feasts. Now over 3,000 of them, mostly poor, rural Indians had gathered to say goodbye. The next day, his body would be flown back to be laid to rest in the little country cemetery of Okarche, Oklahoma. But in accordance with the burial customs of the Tzutuhil Indians, his heart would be buried underneath the altar of the little village church in Santiago de Atitlan. Today a headstone marks his grave site in the Oklahoma countryside. His parents, Frank and Gertrude, had these words inscribed in the granite stone, Stanley Rother–"Padre Aplas." For some months prior to his murder, Stan Rother knew that he, like Peter the fisherman, would have to stretch out his arms and be led to a place where he did not want to go. The warnings of villagers, coworkers, and family had not been able to dissuade him from returning to his flock in time to preside at Holy Week services. Knowing that perhaps the terrifying knock of his tormentors would come in the middle of the night as he lay sleeping, he had taken to the habit of going to bed fully clothed, so that if need be he could escape into the night at a moment's notice. Perhaps compelled by an even greater fear that harm could come to his parishioners if he tried to escape, Stan was willing to submit himself over to the will of God.

Surrendering to the will of God is also a powerful theme throughout the life of Jesus. For example, the gospel writers record that Jesus had to confront an experience of terror near the end of his own life. A number of times before his arrest, trial and execution, he told his own disciples that he would have to face a terrible death. And so, we read that it was in the Garden of Gethsemane, before his arrest, that he prayed, "Father," he said, "if you will, take this cup of suffering away from me. Not my will, however, but your will be done."[3] Ironically, some thirty-three years before Gethsemane, a young Jewish woman, her heart trembling with fear, in response to the message of an angel that she would conceive and bear a son, uttered similar words in a prayer that said, "I am the Lord's servant, may it happen to me as you have said."[4] In this sense, Jesus' prayer in the Garden of Gethsemane reminds us of the prayer once uttered by his mother at the time of his conception.

From the time that I was just a little boy, I, too, learned a prayer of surrendering to God by heart; although, growing up, I never really grasped the depth of its meaning. Often I have said the prayer in silence, sometimes in worship, other times in joy, in sorrow, or somewhere in between. But, always I have repeated it, mindful that it was the first prayer taught to me by my mother. In part it says, "thy will be done: on earth as it is in heaven." For the longest time, the part of the Lord's Prayer that struck me as the most difficult to put into practice seemed to me to be the part that says, "and forgive us our trespasses, as we forgive those who trespass against us." However, the older I get, and the longer I live, I am now of the opinion that the hardest part to put into practice is, "your will be done." After all, this requires me to begin and end each and every day with the realization that God, not I, is ultimately in control of all that I am, and all that I seek to do.

A LITTLE BOY TRUSTS HIS MOTHER

A story is told about another little boy in *The Christian's Secret of a Happy Life* by Hannah Whitall Smith. It goes like this:

A Christian lady was once expressing to a friend how impossible she found it to say, "Thy will be done," and how afraid she would be to do it. She was the mother of an only little boy, who was the heir to a great fortune, and the idol of her heart. After she had stated her difficulties fully, her friend said, "Suppose your little Charley should come running to you tomorrow and say, 'Mother I have made up my mind to let you have your own way with me from this time forward. I am always going to obey you, and I want you to do just whatever you think best with me. I will trust your love.' "How would you feel towards him? Would you say to yourself, 'Ah, now I have a chance to make Charley miserable? I will take away all his pleasures, and fill his life with every hard and disagreeable thing that I can find. I will compel him to do just the things that are the most difficult for

him to do, and will give him all sorts of impossible commands.'
"Oh, no, no, no!" exclaimed the indignant mother. "You know
I would not. You know I would hug him to my heart and cover
him with kisses, and would hasten to fill his life with all that
was sweetest and best." "And are you more tender and loving
than God?" asked her friend. "Ah no!" was the reply. "I see my
mistake. Of course I must not be any more afraid of saying,
'Thy will be done,' to my heavenly Father than I would want
my Charley to be of saying it to me.[5]

Over time, I have come to understand how difficult it is to say
"Thy will be done" and to be willing to relinquish control of my
life to a loving heavenly Father. I want to be willing, like Peter, the
fisherman, to have a belt tied around my own waist, to be able to
stretch out my arms in complete trust and vulnerability, and to be
willing to be led to a place I would rather not go.

In the summer of 1995 I was appointed by my religious supe-
riors to serve as the leader of the major seminary in San Antonio,
Texas. Under the most normal of circumstances, the most seasoned
and experienced priest would find taking on this responsibility a
most daunting and difficult task. However, my circumstances were
anything but normal. At the age of thirty-four, and only nine years
ordained a priest, I would be the youngest person in the country
to hold this position. In fact, over the five years that I attended
national and regional meetings of rectors of major seminaries in
the United States, often I would be the only person in the entire
room with a full head of black, not gray, hair.

I must confess that, in spite of my inexperience and shortcom-
ings, many of my colleagues turned out to be very supportive and
encouraging. A good number of them went out of their way to
include me and make me feel welcomed. Their acceptance made
my job easier, because, over time, it made me feel that I must
be up to the task if they were willing to include me so readily.
Nevertheless, there were many days when I struggled to trust and

relinquish control of my situation to God. In my mind, I believed I was trusting God, but often I would slip back into the pattern of trying to control and micromanage people and the outcomes of a variety of situations. Often I would say, "thy will be done," however, I would hope that God would do my will, instead.

During those difficult years as leader of the seminary, one of the most important revelations I had was coming across a prayer, in a book of prayers that I photocopied and read daily. I began to stick it in my shirt pocket every morning at the start of each day before heading out the front door of my residence. Even after I committed the prayer to memory, I would still carry a copy of the prayer in my pocket every day, as a constant reminder of the need to submit my will over to the will of God. The prayer says simply:

> The supreme good is like water, which nourishes all things without trying to. It is content with the low places that people disdain. Thus it is like the Tao. In dwelling, live close to the ground. In thinking, keep to the simple. In conflict, be fair and generous. In governing, don't try to control. In work, do what you enjoy. In family life, be completely present. When you are content to be simply yourself, and don't compare or compete, everybody will respect you.[6]

Often, during the course of a day, I would pause and read the prayer over and over again. Many times my eyes would gravitate toward the line that says, "In governing don't try to control." Over time, I decided that I would try to do my best in my new job, and then leave the rest up to God. One day while walking across the seminary campus, I stopped and read these words inscribed on a bronze marker, "ESTABLISHED IN 1915." At that moment it occurred to me that the seminary had been in existence long before I got there, long before I was even born. Ultimately, it would continue to exist, and flourish, long after I was gone and someone else would be appointed to take my place. Hence, I decided that all God was asking me to do was to do my very best according to my own human abilities and human limitations.

Due in large measure to the little prayer, I decided I would try to give control over many of life's daily struggles to God. When it came to my work and ministry, I decided I would trust my colleagues and seminary students to do their jobs. I would support and encourage them, and then stay out of their way, unless they needed me. I decided, then and there, that God would provide, if I was first willing to place my trust in God. When the time came for the Board of Trustees of the Seminary to conduct a review of my job performance, fortunately, I was given a positive review. But, as I look back on that experience, I never would have been able to succeed were it not for the words of the little prayer, "The supreme good is like water...it nourishes all things without trying to..."

THE ROPE THAT BINDS

In our lives, giving control of most of our daily struggles over to God is not something that comes naturally. Often our basic human instinct is to want to exert control over even the smallest things in daily life. From the brand of toothpaste I will use in the mornings to the kind of breakfast cereal I will eat before leaving for work, to the style of clothing I will wear, to the kind of pillow I will lay my head upon at bedtime, every fiber of my being seems to long for the capacity to control and govern my basic human needs. And yet, the words of Jesus to Peter, "someday they will tie a belt around your waist and lead you where you do not want to go" are words also spoken to you and to me, and to every believer who seeks to hear the voice of Jesus and put into practice his vision for living.

At first glance, the experience of being led to a place where we do not wish to go seems more appropriate for the elderly and invalid, who, spending the last years of their life in a nursing home, must be pushed in a wheelchair to go from room to room. They are too weak to resist the cords of their years and the burden of their illnesses. Their lethargy makes it impossible for them to walk from place to place. Sometimes such nursing home residents are even tied in restraints, in order that they do not fall and break a hip. Sometimes, because they are so vulnerable, surveillance cameras are installed in their rooms to ensure that no one does them harm in their state of complete vulnerability. But the experience of being led where we do not wish to go does not apply solely to the physically vulnerable. The passage is not intended to apply to every human situation, nor is it meant to suggest that we should give up trying to control certain aspects of our daily lives. As a youth I quickly learned the old adage that came from the lips of many a teacher, coach, and elder that often reminded me that the Lord helps those who are willing to first help themselves.

Therefore, persons with a drinking problem, who wish to overcome the addiction, struggle to regain control over their impulse to drink too much. If they fail to do so, they, along with their family or loved ones, will suffer the negative consequences of alcoholism. Parents will work to instill a sense of discipline and respect in their child from an early age; otherwise they will lose control over the child's behavior. We have heard it said by sports authorities that the world's greatest athletes have a remarkable capacity to control their emotions and to govern their emotional range. Hence, it is said that the great golfer, Tiger Woods, is able to filter out many of the distractions on a golf course. This ability to govern his emotional range, joined with his enormous natural talent, separates Tiger from the rest of the pack. So, while there are certain things we can control and should control, at times every human being is faced with the task of discerning and judging when it is appropriate and healthy for us to control and govern certain aspects of our lives, and when someone, or something, will come along and tie a belt around our waist and take us to a place we do not want to go.

In his wonderful book, *The Holy Longing*, Ron Rolheiser employs a powerful metaphor to describe the experience of being led to a place we do not want to go. He calls this dimension of the Christian life the "rope of conscription." For instance, when a young married couple begins to have children and raise a family, it is like a "rope" that is placed around them, compelling them to make choices and sacrifices no longer based on their own self-interest as a couple alone, but rather, based on what is in the best interest of their family and children. He describes in further detail the "rope of conscription" placed around the married couple in this way:

> Instead of their normal agenda, they are conscriptivley, asked to make a lot of sacrifices in terms of lifestyle, career, hobbies, meals out, vacations, travel, and so on. Their children stand before them daily, like Jesus before Peter, asking: "Do you love me?" If the parents say "yes," then, biblically speaking, the children reply: "Up until now, you have girded your belts and walked wherever you wanted to, but now we are putting a rope around you and taking you where you rather not go, namely, out of your natural selfishness and into self-sacrificing maturity.[7]

A DISTANT SHORE, A VOICE, AND A LOVELY FACE

To borrow for a moment Ron Rolheiser's metaphor of the "conscriptive rope," I'm reminded of a personal family example where such a "rope" or belt was tied around my collective family. This occurred when the time came for us to say goodbye to my dying mother. Over the course of sixty-one years of marriage, she and my father had raised thirteen children, who in turn had given them over sixty grandchildren and great-grandchildren. As the time of my mother's death approached, our family began to realize that we had little control over the amount of suffering she would endure, much less when death would finally come.

For several months the cumulative effects of congestive heart failure, crippling rheumatoid arthritis, dementia, and glaucoma had converged to create a slow and painstaking journey toward death. For the last fourteen days of her time with us, she was a tiny eighty-five pounds, reduced to swallowing gulps of baby formula as her only form of nourishment. For hours and days at a time her children and grandchildren would take turns at her bedside at home, trying to provide as much comfort, care, and love as was humanly possible. For a time we prayed that she might be healed and restored to health, but then, in a way that can only be fully understood by someone who has had a similar experience of watching someone you love suffer, our prayer was transformed into a collective, "Your will, O God, not my will be done." Just as Jesus prayed in the Garden of Gethsemane, just as Mary prayed, in fear and trembling, before the angel, just as Stan Rother prayed when the knock came after midnight in Santiago de Atitlan, now it was our turn to pray, to trust and to give control over to God.

A belt had been tied around us. A "conscriptive rope" was taking us where we did not want to go. Someone we loved deeply and unconditionally was slowly dying before our eyes, and we couldn't do a single thing to change the outcome. In the end, all we could do was love. In retrospect, the only thing we had any control over was the depth of love we would offer my mother at her bedside. Whether it was softly singing her favorite lullaby, touching her parched lips with a moist cloth, nursing her bed sores, or just saying over and over again, "I love you, Mom," all we could control was how we would continue to love her in her final days. In the end, a belt around us was pulling where we did not want to go. And we were being asked to trust that healing and rest would come for my mother, in a way, and in a place, that we could not see, much less, fully understand. The belt around our waist beckoned us, in a way that was gentle, yet firm, that it was time to trust and let go of someone we loved.

Over the years, I have often thought back to those days around my mother's bedside. What I did not realize at that particular moment, which I often think of now, was that another belt, one that we could not see, had also been placed around my mother's waist. Gently, yet firmly, the hand of God was tugging and pulling, taking Mom to another place, perhaps where she did not want to go. It's ironic to me, that often when I think of Mom, I picture her in our family kitchen. I see her smiling and cooking for us, as only she could do. And always I see her wearing one of her favorite aprons. For so many years she would tie the apron strings around herself as a beautiful sign of love and devotion to her family. But when the time would come for her to die, she would no longer be able to dress herself and go wherever she wanted.

I believe that the words of Jesus, once spoken to Peter at daybreak on a distant shore, in a distant land, will be repeated many times over to us and to those we love throughout the course of our own lives. Like Peter, like Stan Rother, like my mother, many times we will hear these words, and we will be invited to stretch out our arms as a sign of our own trust, vulnerability, and confidence in God. Perhaps, we, too, will be invited to go to a place where we do not want to go. If at those particular moments, I am willing to trust beyond my fears, my apprehensions, my sorrows, and my doubts, I believe that I will catch a glimpse, if only for a moment, of what lies beyond the horizon. There, on another distant shore, I will hear again the voice of him who beckoned me, and then I will see with my own eyes the lovely face of God.

Chapter II

Mercy Has a Face

The corporate model of religion can get along quite well without any real transformation or learning how to live in the fire. As others have said, there are two common doorways into the world of religion. One doorway has "Salvation" written on it; the other has "Discussions about salvation" written on it. You can be ordained a priest or even a bishop, living a whole life in the discussion room and, even worse, merely trying to control the discussion. You can avoid the messenger your whole life by making orthodox distinctions about the message. The world is tired of us talking about Jesus. Now we must be Jesus. As Francis told his friars, preach the gospel at all times, and when necessary use words.[8]

SHARING CHOCOLATE

A story is told about a little boy who unexpectedly encountered Jesus while walking home one day from Sunday school. Having just learned an important lesson the little boy decides to share his chocolate bar with someone in need. The story goes like this:

A young boy was walking home through the park after attending a Sunday school class. Somehow, he couldn't stop thinking about the lesson for that day on Jesus' parable of the last judgment. What impressed him most was when the teacher said, when you give something to another person, you're really giving it to Jesus. As he continued through the park, he noticed an old women sitting on a bench. She looked lonely and hungry. So he sat down next to her, took from his pocket a chocolate bar he had been saving and offered some to her. She accepted with a smile. He liked her smile so much that after she had eaten her piece of chocolate he gave her more. This time they exchanged smiles and, for a while, they sat together in silence, just smiling at each other. Finally, the boy got up to leave. As he began to walk away, he turned, ran back to the bench, and gave the woman a big hug. And she gave him her very best smile. When he arrived home, his mother saw a big smile on his face and asked. "What made you so happy today?" He said, "I shared my chocolate bar with Jesus. And she has a great smile." Meanwhile, the old woman returned to her little apartment where she lived with her sister. "You're all smiles, "said the sister. "What made you so happy today?" To which she replied, "I was sitting in the park, eating a chocolate bar with Jesus. And, you know, he looks a lot younger than I expected."[9]

The story of the little boy illustrates an important dimension of the Christian faith. That is, we are to seek and discover the person of Jesus that is abiding in every person we encounter throughout the course of our daily lives. Discovering or recognizing the person and presence of Jesus in others is not a matter of picking and choosing, but rather a matter of awareness. In other words, the living, breathing presence of the Risen Jesus is there in every person we meet, provided we are willing to look beyond the ordinary physical characteristics of the person we encounter.

THE MESSIAH AND THE MONKS

Similarly, we Christians believe and hope that others will come to recognize the living presence of Jesus in us. To put it another way, if I encounter you, the Christ in you will reveal himself to me, while the Christ in me will reveal himself to you. How different the world (and our lives) would be if only we could embrace this ideal. Would I treat others more gently and respectfully? How would others treat me? How would this change the world? A parable that further underscores this point is worth noting.

High in the mountains was a monastery that had once been known throughout the world. Its monks were pious; its students were enthusiastic. The chants from the monastery's chapel deeply touched the hearts of those who came there to meditate and to pray. But something changed. Fewer and fewer young men came to study there; fewer and fewer people came for spiritual nourishment. The monks who remained became disheartened and sad. Deeply worried, the abbot of the monastery went off in search of an answer. Why had his monastery fallen on such hard times? The abbot went to a wise master, and he asked, "Is it because of some sin of ours that our monastery is no longer full of vitality?" "Yes," replied the master. "It is the sin of ignorance." "The sin of ignorance?" questioned the abbot. "Of what are we ignorant?" The wise master looked at the abbot for a long time, and then he said, "One of you is the messiah in disguise. But you are all ignorant of this." The master closed his eyes, and he was silent. "The messiah?" thought the abbot. "The messiah is one of us? Who could it be? We are all so flawed; we are all so full of faults. Isn't the messiah supposed to be perfect?" "But, then," thought the abbot, "perhaps his faults are part of his disguise. So which one of us could it be? Could it be Brother Cook? Brother Treasurer? Brother Bell Ringer? Brother Vegetable Grower? Which one? Which one?" When the abbot returned to the monastery, he gathered all the monks together and told them what the wise master had said. "One of us? The messiah? Impossible!" But the master had spoken, and the master was never wrong. "One of us? The messiah? Incredible! But it must be so. Which one? Which one could it be? That brother over there? That one? That one?" Not knowing who among them was the messiah; all the monks began treating one another with new respect. "You never know," they thought, "he might be the one, or he might be the one, so I had better deal with each and every one of them kindly. I will speak gentle words. I will be considerate and helpful. I will give everyone the utmost honor. I will smile and be pleasant all the time." It was not long before the monastery was filled with new found joy. Soon new students came to learn, and people came from far and wide to be inspired by the chants of the kind, smiling monks. And once again the monastery was filled with the spirit of love, the spirit of God.

In the story, the monks, began to recognize the presence of the messiah in each other, yet it is worthwhile to note that the idea of recognizing the Risen Jesus is one area that the authors of the New Testament had difficulty describing. For instance in the gospel of Luke, Jesus appears to the disciples in Jerusalem and declares to them "Peace be with you!" Unfortunately, or perhaps by design, the disciples thought that they were seeing a ghost. Hence, Jesus reassures them that he is not a ghost. "Why are you alarmed? Why are these doubts coming up in your minds?" he says. And as if to reassure them even further that it is really he, he continues, "Look at my hands and my feet, and see that it is I myself. Feel me, and you will know, for a ghost doesn't have flesh and bones, as you can see I have."[10]

Another time when the disciples do not immediately recognize the Risen Jesus can be found earlier in the same chapter of Luke's gospel. This episode takes place on the road to the town of Emmaus located seven miles northwest of the City of Jerusalem. Walking along the road, two of Jesus' disciples were discussing the events they had witnessed surrounding the crucifixion and death of Jesus of Nazareth, when a "stranger" approached them along the way. According to Luke, the gospel writer, "As they talked and discussed, Jesus himself drew near and walked along with them; they saw him, but somehow did not recognize him."[11] Similarly, in the gospel of John, the Risen Jesus appears to Mary Magdalen while she is weeping outside his tomb. At first glance Mary believes that she is speaking to the gardener, until Jesus calls her by name, and Mary embraces him crying out, "Teacher!"[12]

HE KEPT HIS IDENTITY SECRET

The idea that we do not always recognize Jesus at first glance or that Jesus sometimes keeps his true identity secret is illustrated in the parable of the sheep and the goats. The gospel of Matthew records that on judgment day the sheep and the goats will be separated. On that day the king will say to the wicked, "Away from me, you that are under God's curse! Away to the eternal fire which has been prepared for the Devil and his angels! I was hungry but you would not feed me, thirsty but you would not give me a drink; I was a stranger but you would not welcome me in your homes, naked but you would not clothe me; I was sick and in prison but you would not take care of me."[13]

In this beautiful commentary on the parable of judgment day in Matthew's gospel, William Barclay has noted:

This is one of the most vivid parables Jesus ever spoke, and the lesson is crystal clear—that God will judge us in accordance with our reaction to human need. His judgment does not depend on the knowledge we have amassed, or the fame that we have acquired, or the fortune that we have gained, but on the help that we have given…The things which Jesus picks out—giving a hungry man a meal or a thirsty man a drink, welcoming a stranger, cheering the sick, visiting the prisoner—are things which anyone can do…Those who helped did not think they were helping Christ and thus piling up eternal merit…Whereas, on the other hand, the attitude of those who failed to help was; "If we had known it was *you* we would gladly have helped; but we thought it was only some common man who was not worth helping."[14]

Barclay goes on to further explain in simple, yet compelling terms, the idea of helping Jesus himself when we help another by adding:

> Jesus confronts us with the wonderful truth that all such help given is given to himself, and all such help withheld is withheld from himself. How can that be? If we really wish to delight a parent's heart, if we really wish to move him to gratitude, the best way to do it is to help his child. God is the great Father; and the way to delight the heart of God is to help his children, our fellow-men.[15]

An example of Jesus' keeping his true identity secret from a believer is found in a story from the 4th century about St. Martin of Tour, a Roman soldier and a Christian. One cold winter day as he was entering a city, a beggar stopped him and asked for alms. Martin had no money, but the beggar was blue and shivering with cold and Martin gave what he had. He took off his soldier's coat worn and frayed as it was, cut it in two and gave half of it to the beggar. That night he had a dream. In it he saw the heavenly places and all the angels with Jesus in the midst of them. Jesus was wearing half of a Roman soldier's cloak. One of the angels said to him, "Master, why are you wearing that battered old cloak? Who gave it to you?" Jesus answered softly, "My servant Martin gave it to me."[16]

A PRISONER BECOMES A SAINT

One who did not fail to recognize the presence of the Risen Jesus in others was Maximilian Kolbe, a Polish priest living near the village of Warsaw during the height of Hitler's systematic genocide of the Jews and other undesirables to the Nazi regime. Not counting the cost to himself, he stood up for what he believed to be right and just. After being falsely accused, for crimes he did not commit, he was imprisoned in Auschwitz, a Nazi concentration camp. There, along with other innocent victims of the Holocaust, Maximilian was subjected to some of the most terrible idignities known to man. Perhaps films, such as *Sophie's Choice* or *Schindler's List* convey some of the pain, humiliation, and despair suffered by millions at the hands of the Nazis, but ultimately, these films and others like them can never fully do justice to the true horrors of the holocaust.

According to a number of sources, Maximilian and his companions were assigned to cut down trees so that badly needed lumber could be used for the war. Often malnourished, kicked, beaten and tortured, they worked under the most trying of circumstances. But, in spite of these conditions it seems that Maximilian continued to be a source of inspiration and consolation for his fellow prisoners. At times he would even try to offer the prayers of the Mass for other Catholic prisoners whenever they could smuggle bread and wine inside the prison walls.

In the summer of 1941 Maximilian offered to exchange his life for the life of a man about to be executed when the commandant of the concentration camp ordered the execution of ten prisoners after one prisoner had escaped in the night. When Frank Gajowniczek, one of the ten men about to be executed, cried out in despair that he would never again see his wife and children, Maximilian came forward and said, "I am a Catholic priest. I wish to die for that man. I am old; he has a wife and children."[17] Days later, Maximilian, and the other condemned men, died when they were starved to death as a deterrent to prevent further escapes.

When John Paul II elevated Maximilian Kolbe to sainthood, in attendance at the ceremony, where the canonization took place, was Frank Gajowniczek, the man whose life Maximilian had saved. In the face of modern day atrocities and man's inhumanity to man stands the remarkable example of the simple and humble priest. In a place so marked by the stench of fear and death, he summoned within himself the God-given goodness and charity of heart that allowed him to lay down his life for another. It is that same God-given goodness and mercy that is at work in the heart of a young woman willing to donate a kidney to her brother in order that he may live. It is at work in the heart of a mother who refuses to believe that her nineteen year old will never walk again as a result of a head injury. Thus, she devotes herself to being his nurse and therapist so that someday he may walk again. It is at work in the heart of an elderly retired couple who sacrifice their golden years of retirement in order to devote themselves to a middle-aged son, who as a result of a tumor in this throat, is consigned to a breathing machine for the rest of his life. These are not hypothetical examples formed out of a vivid imagination. Rather, they are but a few of the examples from real life witnessed almost weekly, if not daily, by people like me fortunate enough to be in a position of caring for others.

Recall the story of the young boy who shared his chocolate bar with Jesus. He kept thinking about the Sunday school lesson he had learned that day, "When you give something to another person you're really giving it to Jesus." We will never know to what degree Maximilian Kolbe thought that in exchanging his life for his fellow prisoner, he was really doing something for Jesus. We can only speculate that he would have known and thought about the lesson of the last judgment many times over the course of his life. "When Lord, did I see you naked, and clothe you…When did I see you hungry and thirsty and give you food and drink…When Lord did I see you in prison, and visit you? When did I see you weeping and wipe the tears from your cheeks? When did I see you grieving for the loss of your loved one and console you with a loving embrace? When did I see your heart breaking with sorrow and speak words of comfort and compassion?" And, perhaps the Lord spoke softly to Maximilian, deep within the recesses of his heart, "As often as you did it for one of the least of your brothers and sisters, Maximilian, you did it for me."

LORD GIVE ME SOMEONE

An awesome and moving prayer, *Lord Give Me Someone,* captures the essence of what it means to love unselfishly, without counting the cost, and seeing the Risen Jesus in the least of our brothers and sisters:

Lord,
When I am famished, give me someone who needs food;
When I am thirsty, send me someone who needs water;
When I am cold, send me someone to warm
When I am hurting, send me someone to console;
When my cross becomes heavy, give me another's cross to share;
When I am poor, lead someone needy to me;
When I have no time, give me someone to help for a moment;
When I am humiliated, give me someone to praise;
When I am discouraged, send me someone to encourage;
When I need another's understanding, give me someone who needs mine;
When I need someone to take care of me, send me someone to care for.
When I think of myself, turn my thoughts to another.[18]

Even under the most desperate of circumstances, Maximilian was able to see the presence of the Risen Jesus in the least of his brothers and sisters in Auschwitz. In the prayer, "Lord Give Me Someone," the challenge is to do likewise, even under the most trying of circumstances in our own lives. To recognize the presence of the Risen Jesus in others is not always going to be easy, especially in the times of our own lives when we are weary, tired, lonely, sick, depressed, or discouraged. After all, it is only human to think of ourselves first during difficult and trying times. But, to turn our thoughts to the needs of another, when our impulse is to think only of ourselves, requires a special kind of grace. And, I believe that the "potential" for that special grace is residing in each and every one of us. I am so certain of this, that I think it is fair to say that the "unrealized grace" that is within us that ultimately enables us to recognize the presence of the Risen Jesus in others, is none other than the presence of Jesus, himself. It is the living, breathing presence of the Risen Jesus that he promised would be with us, as he put it, "And I will be with you always, to the end of the age."[19]

GRITS AND SPIRITUAL DNA

This special grace is such an essential part of our character that it is virtually impossible for us to forfeit it. It is, as it were, part and parcel of our "spiritual DNA." To be sure, it is sometimes dormant or obscured by our unwillingness to draw upon it, but nevertheless, once we are endowed with it, it is there just waiting for us to "summon it" and put it to good use. The author of *The Road Less Traveled and Beyond*, M. Scott Peck, gives a very practical and yet profound example of this pervasive quality of grace. From his perspective, "grace" and "gratitude" are qualities of the human person that share a special relationship.

> If something is earned it is not a true gift. Grace, however, is unearned. It is free. It is gratis. The words grace, gratis, and gratitude flow into one another. If you perceive grace, you will naturally feel grateful. A story told to me by a famous preacher involved a young Yankee, who, on a business trip, had to drive through the South for the first time in his life. He had driven all night and was in a hurry. By the time he arrived in South Carolina, he was really hungry. Stopping at a roadside diner, he ordered a breakfast of scrambled eggs and sausage, and was taken by surprise when his order came back and there was a white blob of something on the plate. "What's that?" he asked the waitress. "Thems grits, suh," she replied in her strong southern accent.

"But I didn't order them," he said. "You don't order grits," she responded. "They just come." And that said the preacher, is very much like grace. You don't order it. It just comes.[20]

And so it is that grace, and the capacity, or potential to recognize the presence of the living, breathing Risen Jesus in others is residing within each of us. Although, as previously mentioned, sometimes it is not so easy to summon the gift and put it to use. It is especially difficult to recognize and see Jesus in the other, when that other is truly one of the "least" of God's children.

FEEDING CHUCK AND BEING FED

Perhaps the following personal example will further illustrate what I mean. It is a tale of two friends, Tony and Chuck, both dear to me. The three of us were among a group of American students studying theology in Europe during the early 1980's in preparation for ordination to the priesthood. For four years we lived, breathed, and ate theology at the great University of Louvain in Belgium near the heart of Central Europe. Our hope, as was the hope of all of our classmates, was to study and prepare in this beautiful but rigorous setting, and then return to our homeland, the United States, where we would then proceed to "save the world." While Tony and I went on to begin our careers in the priesthood, Chuck made a decision early in his training that he would return to the United States and resume a successful career in the world of finance and business.

To this day it is very easy for me to recognize the presence of the Risen Jesus in my friend, Tony. From the time we were young seminarians to the present day, I see and feel in Tony the living, breathing presence of the person of Jesus. Whether we are enjoying a baseball game or sitting around the dining room table of his mother's home enjoying a sumptuous Italian dinner, I see Tony, and then I see Jesus. It is as if they (Jesus and Tony) are one and the same. On the other hand, the experience of trying to recognize the Risen Jesus in my friend, Chuck, has not been so easy. In the fall of 1989, I traveled from Texas to New Jersey to pay Tony a visit and from there I traveled to Bridgeport, Connecticut to visit Chuck. The first few days in New Jersey with Tony, his family, and other wonderful friends were delightful and lighthearted, while the latter part of the journey was painful and gut wrenching. Before leaving Texas, I had received word from an alumnus of the seminary that Chuck, our classmate, had been diagnosed with AIDS. Chuck, he said, had asked him to call me and let me know of his condition since he had always considered me to be among his closest friends. To be sure, as classmates, we had been privileged during our time in Europe to accumulate some very happy memories. Looking back, I believe all of us bonded together more closely since our families were thousands of miles away back home. Years of praying together, sharing meals, traveling to different countries, and simply supporting each other through difficult times really made us all feel like brothers. Now, one of the "brothers" was very sick and likely to die.

Because in 1989, a great deal was still unknown about AIDS, and thus, a terrible stigma was attached to the disease, I was very nervous the day I arrived at the hospital in Bridgeport. Clumsily I greeted Chuck, Chuck's mother, and Chuck's significant other who was caring for him during the final stages of his illness. For the next couple of days I struggled over what to say and what to do to ease my friend's pain. He was not the Chuck I had known and loved back in seminary days. The Chuck back in seminary was joyful, energetic, bright, prayerful, and thoughtful. This Chuck was down to 120 pounds of his former self. This Chuck was frail and partially paralyzed. Gone was the Chuck I had known and whose company I had enjoyed just a few short years before.

But in the span of those short few days in Bridgeport something unexpected and somewhat mysterious came over me. As I sat next to Chuck's hospital bed for hours at a time, as I heard his voice, as we remembered and laughed about old times, as we sang songs we had once sung in our seminary chapel, as we talked well into the night, as we prayed for strength and healing, something was beginning to stir inside of me. Slowly, somewhat painstakingly, I realized that if I could not see Jesus in my friend Chuck, I would never truly be able to see Jesus in anyone else in my life. It soon occurred to me, pacing the hospital floor of that Connecticut hospital that it was no accident that I had come to know Chuck in the first place. Indeed, God was putting me through the acid test. Could I really see and love Jesus in one of the least of his children or was everything I had ever preached to people about seeing Christ in others just pietistic drivel?

As the day of my departure drew near, I could hear the sound of sadness in Chuck's voice that I would soon be leaving to go back to Texas. But I could also hear the sound of gratitude that I had gone to be at his side, even if it was only for a few short days. On the day of my departure, I fed Chuck some spoonfuls of chocolate pudding. With tears in his eyes, with slurred speech, he said, "Thank you, for feeding me." Later that day, when it came time to say goodbye, I embraced Chuck, and he embraced me. Looking back, I now realize that at that moment the Jesus in me was embracing the Jesus in him, while the Jesus in him was embracing the Jesus in me.

SHE COMFORTED THE HUMAN FACE OF GOD

Two months later, on New Years Eve, I learned from a phone call from one of our seminary classmates that Chuck had passed away earlier that afternoon. In all the years that have passed since that October day when I embraced my friend at his bedside, not one New Year's Eve has gone by when I don't think of my good friend and seminary brother. I often remember the words he spoke to me, "Thank you for feeding me." Often, over the years, when I look back on that fall of 1989, I recall that in many churches there is an image that is displayed among other images. These fourteen "stations" are particular moments in Jesus' life as he journeyed to the place where he was nailed to a cross between two thieves on a hillside overlooking Jerusalem. Customarily, one of those stations or images evokes the memory of a woman who lovingly and courageously wiped the face of Jesus as he carried his cross to Calvary. This woman, Veronica, lovingly comforted the human face of God by wiping away his blood, his sweat and his tears. It was not an act of miraculous proportions, only a single act of love and mercy. It was a gesture not limited to a particular time and place, an act not frozen in time; rather, it was a gesture worth repeating over and over again. When? When will we ever wipe your face, O Lord? How often he must say to us, deep within the recesses of our own hearts, "As often as you wipe the face of one of the least of my children, you do it again, for me."

Chapter III

Compassion Has a Face

I have come to Yad Vashem to pay homage to the millions of Jewish people, who stripped of everything, especially their human dignity, were murdered in the Holocaust. We wish to remember. But to remember for a purpose, namely to ensure that never again will evil prevail, as it did for millions of innocent victims of Nazism. There are no words strong enough to deplore the personal tragedy of the Shoa. Jews and Christians share an immense spiritual patrimony…our teachings demand that we overcome evil with good. Let us build a new future in which there will be no more anti-Jewish feeling among Christians, or anti-Christian feeling among Jews, but rather the mutual respect required of those who adore the one Creator and Lord, and look to Abraham as our common father in faith.[21]

A POPE LIGHTS A FLAME

These moving words were spoken on March 23, 2000, by Pope John Paul II to survivors of the Jewish Holocaust at Yad Vashem Holocaust Memorial on the occasion of his historic visit to Israel. After lighting the eternal flame, the Pope met with a number of Polish Jews in attendance who had survived the horrors of the concentration camps. One of those survivors, Edith Zirer, spoke eloquently about her experience of being liberated from the camp in 1945. "After the years in the camp I was totally weakened by tuberculosis and other ailments that left me virtually paralyzed. A young Karol Wojtyla carried me on his shoulders for two miles from the concentration camp to the railroad station where I joined other survivors. He gave me a sandwich and bowl of soup." After staying in a Krakow orphanage, and later in a French sanatorium, in 1951 she emigrated to Israel where she married. Now over 50 years later, Edith stood at Yad Vashem with Karol Wojtyla, now John Paul II, to pay homage to the 6 million Jews who did not survive the Shoa.

The historic visit of the Pope to the holocaust memorial in Jerusalem prompted one newspaper headline to read, "Pope Pours Oil Over Old Wounds." An editorial in the most widely read newspaper in Israel said of the papal visit, "Mercy has come to the State of Israel this week, and has left politics to one side. A religion that once spilt blood with the Crusades and the Inquisition, has become a religion in which its priests are raised to the level of the just among nations."[22]

Reading the accounts of the Pope's visit to Yad Vashem, and his remarks to the Holocaust survivors, I was struck by the headline, "Pope Pours Oil Over Old Wounds." It occurred to me that headline speaks volumes to what every believer in Jesus should be about in his or her daily life. To pour oil over old wounds, to restore and heal broken relationships, to find ways to impart renewed energy and strength where there is hurt, anger or despair, each of us in our own relationships, and our own particular setting, is called to pour oil over the wounds we encounter in the lives of others and in our own lives.

Writing to people who had suffered the collective and individual wounds of captivity, where they, like the Jews in the concentration camps, had been stripped of their human dignity by their captors, Isaiah, the Hebrew prophet, speaks these words of hope and healing. "The Sovereign Lord has filled me with his spirit. He has chosen me and sent me to bring good news to the poor, to heal the broken-hearted, to announce release to captives and freedom to those in prison…He has sent me to comfort all who mourn, to give to those who mourn in Zion joy and gladness instead of grief, a song of praise instead of sorrow."[23]

A VILLAIN BECOMES A HERO

How are we to go about the work of healing the brokenhearted, of pouring out on others the oil of gladness? In a story recorded only in the Gospel of Luke, Jesus gives an example of one who unexpectedly was called upon to become a source of healing for another. It is a story that applies to every culture, every religion, and every age. Its power and meaning are intended to be a model of how we are to love and how we are to put the needs of others before our own needs. The story is one of the most compelling and inspirational stories ever told. Throughout the centuries, many have come to know it as the story of the Good Samaritan.

In it, Jesus tells of a man who had been badly beaten by robbers and left for dead by the side of the road. Seemingly, the situation appears hopeless until an "outsider" traveling the lonely road to Jericho, stops to render aid. Two others before him, both religious authorities, fail to stop, fearing perhaps that contact with a corpse would render them unclean for temple duty. It is the Samaritan instead who becomes a source of healing. Remember that the story is told after a lawyer poses a question to Jesus about what he must do to inherit eternal life. "What do the Scriptures say? How do you interpret them?" Jesus asked him. In response, he answered, "Love the Lord your God with all your heart, with all your soul, with all your strength, and with all your mind; and love your neighbor as you love yourself." Jesus then says to the man, "You are right. Do this and you will live." Perhaps feeling a bit smug that he had answered correctly, the lawyer then asks Jesus, "Who is my neighbor?"[24] It is this question that initiates the telling of the story.

Ultimately, the intention of the story is to contrast the behavior of two authority figures normally held up by society as examples of moral correctness, to that of the behavior of the outcast who would have been despised by the average pious Jew. While the temple authorities observe the "letter of the law," but ignore the wounded man, the example of the Samaritan, who lived outside of the law, is held up by Jesus as the true neighbor to the wounded man. It is safe to conclude that the original hearers of the story would have been shocked, if not outraged, by this "turning of the tables." Would not the typical Jewish audience have expected the hero of the story to be the morally correct priest or Levite? Instead, Jesus applauds the villain.

THE UGLY SAMARITAN

In this regard, Dr. Pheme Perkins provides some very helpful background in her book, *Hearing the Parables of Jesus.* Perkins explains:

"Samaritan" seems to have been a term of insult when applied by one Jew to another…Palestinians living in occupied territory in Israel today have much the same feeling when they see an Israeli soldier that a Jew of the time of Jesus would have had on seeing a Roman one…You need only pick up the newspaper to get a feel for the level of violence in the region. People who live there recognize that the violence with which they live today is part of thousands of years of warfare and suffering in a land where one seems constantly surrounded by enemies.[25]

It appears, from the scholarship available to us from the history of this period, that it is difficult to overemphasize the hostility and animosity that existed between the Samaritans and their Jewish neighbors. To the orthodox Jew, the Samaritans represented illegitimate half-breeds who worshipped foreign gods. Many had intermarried with Gentiles and had abandoned the Jewish practice of worshipping at the Jerusalem temple. This historical background is not simply to belabor the point, but rather to appreciate in a fuller sense how radical and revolutionary Jesus' acceptance of the Samaritans must have appeared to his fellow Jews.

If Jesus' treatment of the Samaritans was likely to have shocked the sensibilities of his fellow Jews, then even more startling to his contemporaries must have been his treatment and acceptance of the Romans. Because the Romans had occupied their land, imposed the burden of taxation, and reigned over them with terror and force, the contempt felt by the Jews for the Samaritans was exceeded only by the contempt they felt for their Roman oppressors. Is it any wonder then that tax collectors who sympathized with and supported the Roman occupation would have been regarded and reviled as being among the worst of public sinners? Nevertheless, Jesus demonstrates on numerous occasions his compassion and mercy for these adversaries of his own people.

The many examples given in the Scriptures of Jesus' treatment and acceptance of those considered enemies by his Jewish brothers and sisters give us a sense of the depth of compassion and empathy that Jesus possessed for those considered to be outcast and outsiders among his own. Consistently his interaction with those considered wicked or wretched is characterized by compassion, mercy, inclusion, and forgiveness. Consistently, the very people so despised and mistreated by the religious and moral establishment are treated with dignity and respect by Jesus.

Nowhere do we see this compassion for others come into focus as clearly as in the account of the Good Samaritan. Here, Jesus offers the Samaritan as the quintessential example of what it is to love. The Samaritan, himself despised and rejected, becomes the vessel of grace and mercy. By treating the wounds of his enemy, Jesus offers him as the example of true compassion and love for his age and for all time.

When we are willing to pattern our own lives after the example of the Samaritan, we will put into practice the commandment given by Jesus to all of his followers, "My commandment is this: love one another, just as I love you. The greatest love you can have for your friends is to give your life for them."[26] The question then becomes, how? How do we become a source of compassion? How do we go about pouring out the oil of mercy upon the wounds and hurts of others? How can we become the oil of compassion and gladness? I began this chapter by remembering the words of John Paul II to the Jewish Holocaust survivors at Yad Vashem. As a young man, in his own homeland, he had carried one of those survivors, Edith Zirer, to a place of safety. More than fifty years later, he spoke to the victims of the Shoa and to the world to help us remember those unspeakable horrors, so that never again should evil prevail. These words were to serve as a remembrance that the spiritual teachings of Christians and Jews demand that we overcome evil with good.

KEEPING A MEMORY ALIVE

Appropriately, Yad Vashem, and other places like it, are often referred to in the English language as "memorials." According to the English definition, a memorial is something like a structure or place that serves to keep alive a memory. Specifically, Yad Vashem is intended to keep alive the memory of the extermination of six million Jews during World War II. Accordingly, it was built to keep that terrible memory alive, in order that evil should not triumph over good; so that good may overcome evil.

Another memorial built to keep alive the memory of a terrible human tragedy is the Oklahoma City National Memorial dedicated to the victims and survivors of the bombing of the Murrah Federal Building on April 19, 1995. The memorial was dedicated and opened to the public five years after the terrible events in 1995 which took 168 lives and seriously injured 600 people. Built directly over the place where so much human destruction and devastation occurred, the memorial is one of the most moving and evocative structures in the country. At an entrance gate erected to overlook the memorial is etched in stone these words:

We come here to remember those who were killed, those who survived and those changed forever. May all who leave here know the impact of violence…May this memorial offer comfort, strength, peace and hope and serenity.[27]

At the center of the memorial is a reflecting pool of water where the original federal building stood. Where so many lost their lives, the water symbolizes life and hope, even in the face of death. On a grassy slope overlooking the reflecting pool are 168 bronze chairs with the names of the men, women, and children that perished in the blast. The empty chairs evoke the sense of loss and emptiness felt by those who lost a loved one or loved ones. To the east of the reflecting pool is a tall and beautiful American Elm that came to be known in the weeks following the explosion, as the "Survivor Tree." The tree came to symbolize the strength and generosity of those countless rescue workers who came to the aid of the injured and wounded, as well as those remarkable individuals who overcame the trauma of their injuries and continued to survive.

One, in Oklahoma City, who like the Good Samaritan, did not count the cost but rather went to tend the wounds of the injured, was Rebecca Anderson, a wife and mother of four. Rebecca, a 37 year old nurse, was not at the site of the explosion on April 19, but hurried into the chaos and rubble after the blast in order to help those who were trapped and could not escape under their own power. While attempting to rescue others at the site, she sustained a serious head wound and died four days later. In trying to save others, Rebecca lost her own life. She became the only rescue worker who was killed in the aftermath of the explosion.

The lessons from the terrible tragedy of Oklahoma City are many. The power of the symbols of the national memorial speak volumes to a modern age, marked exceedingly by violence and a complete disregard for human life. It is hoped that in remembering something so tragic, others may dedicate themselves to putting an end to the violence that has become so commonplace in our society. Otherwise, those who plot evil and do evil, especially to the innocent, will continue to do so and there will be no justice. In fact, it is significant that a museum has been dedicated and opened to the public, adjacent to the national memorial. In large measure, the museum is dedicated to teaching future generations of Americans the effects of violence and terrorism.

So, it is my contention that in an age when we witness, almost daily, the terrible effects of violence, terrorism and war, and a general disregard for the sanctity of human life, the greatest lesson that the symbols of the national memorial have to teach us is that we ourselves must become "living memorials." Like the Good Samaritan, like Rebecca Anderson, we must struggle daily to bring about good where there is evil; to bring about life where there is death and despair. The challenge of the Oklahoma City Memorial is that we must embody the reflecting pool and the survivor tree in our own bodies and in our own hearts. In this way, when we encounter evil and death in our lives, or in the lives of those we love, evil and death will not overwhelm us. Instead, like the majestic elm tree, we will survive the worst life has to offer. And, like Rebecca Anderson, in the midst of sorrow and loss, we will tend the wounds and bring healing to the hurts of our neighbors.

WISH. HOPE. BELIEVE.

If a "living memorial" is one who overcomes evil with good, one who survives the very worst life has to offer, one whose life brings hope and healing where there is death and despair, I can think of no better example than that of Cornelius Abraham. His story is told by Bob Greene, author and columnist for the Chicago Tribune. In the summer of 1987, Cornelius, six years old at the time, and his little brother Lattie, just four, were subjected to child abuse and torture by their mother and her live-in boyfriend, Johnny Campbell.

In the account told by Bob Greene, Campbell repeatedly beat Lattie and burned him with lit cigarettes and a hot iron. Subjecting Cornelius to some of the same abuse, he tied Lattie by his ankles leaving him hanging upside down in a darkened closet. Sticking a rag in his mouth to muffle his screams, he jabbed him with sewing needles and dunked him in scalding hot water. Lattie was subjected to all of this even while he suffered from a broken pelvis and broken collar bone. All the while, the mother of the boys did nothing to stop Campbell as she watched "The Incredible Hulk" on television. On August 14th, Lattie, weighing only 26 pounds, was struck over the head by Campbell, and he collapsed and died. All this was witnessed by Cornelius. Somehow, even though he had been victimized, Cornelius had managed to survive. In the summer of 1990, he was able to testify in court to the murder of his little brother. It was his remarkable courage that sent Johnny Campbell and Alicia Abraham to prison for life.

In recounting the story of Cornelius Abraham, Bob Greene has written that if ever a child could be excused for failing, it was Cornelius. But, instead, the very opposite has come to pass. In the years that have transpired since the summer of 1987, Cornelius has grown up to be as remarkable and courageous a young man as he was as a little boy. Raised by loving foster parents, Dwayne and Ingra Cooper, Cornelius, who studies computer science at Illinois University, was the first recipient of an award established in his honor by the YMCA Network for Counseling and Youth Development of Greater Chicago Land. In making Cornelius the first recipient of the Cornelius S. Abraham Award, officials noted that Cornelius embodies the qualities they hope to instill in children, namely: "Wish. Hope. Believe." In presenting the award to Cornelius, Bob Green said this about his young friend:

Cornelius has had a much more profound effect on my life than I have had on his...He has inspired me from the moment I met him, and that in many ways he is the reason, on my better days, I try to do what I do...His courage in venturing out into a world that conspired to hurt him and hold him down since he was little boy, and his determination not to let that hurt stop him from leading a worthy life, is as impressive as anything I have ever been privileged to witness...he is his little brother's finest legacy.[28]

In overcoming evil with good, in offering hope and life in the face of death and despair, Cornelius is like the majestic elm tree that survived the worst life had to offer. He is an example of a "living memorial," whose life can serve as an inspiration to all who carry the scars and wounds of abuse or neglect from their own childhoods.

The experience suffered by Cornelius Abraham and his little brother Lattie, the experience of the enormous pain and suffering inflicted upon those who died or were injured in the bombing in Oklahoma City, and perhaps, the personal experiences of suffering and loss in our own lives, often pose a very important question about the origin and meaning of suffering. Often, people who are subjected to suffering or sorrow as a result of loss or evil will ask, "Why must I suffer?" "Where is God when I suffer?" "What good can possibly come from suffering?" "Why does God allow this?" While there are a variety of answers to these eternal questions conditioned by one's theological and philosophical world view, the point here is not to digress into a lengthy discourse on the meaning of human suffering. However, neither is it possible to ignore that these questions do come up from time to time in the minds and hearts of many believers. To deny that people pose these, or similar questions about evil or human suffering in the world, is to do a disservice to the intelligent and thoughtful people who fill our churches on Sundays, and who continue to be faithful and loyal to their faith and their beliefs.

I Did Send Help. I Sent You.

In the remaining pages of this chapter I would like to briefly address the point of suffering, albeit, from a very limited perspective. To ensure that my approach is not too theoretical or abstract, I want to address the issue while staying within the framework of the previous discussion of the story of the Good Samaritan. And ultimately, bearing in mind how Jesus tells the story gives us the quintessential example of one whom, although despised by the moral establishment for living outside the law, nevertheless, was neighbor to the man who had been beaten and left for dead. Again, it is noteworthy to remember that Jesus tells the story after his discourse on the most important of the commandments, namely love of God and love of neighbor.

In his book, *Teaching Your Children About God*, David J. Wolpe, includes the following story:

> There is a marvelous story of a man who once stood before God, his heart breaking from the pain and injustice in the world. "Dear God,' he cried out, 'look at all the suffering, the anguish, and distress in your world. Why don't you send help?" God responded, "I did send help. I sent you."[29]

In this little story lies, at least in part, an answer to some of the questions so often posed about the meaning or value of suffering in this world. For example, on the first anniversary of the tragic events of September 11, I happened to come across a newspaper story that posed the question, "Where was God on September 11?" This was not the first time I had heard the question posed in relationship to the events of that terrible day in American history. I believe that the previous story, and God's response, "I did send help. I sent you," provides a helpful answer, in part. Again, drawing upon the events of September 11 to illustrate my point, I believe that on September 11, God was in the persons of Todd

Beamer, Fr. Mychal Judge, and countless others like them. In the case of Todd Beamer, God used this heroic young husband and father, over the skies of Pennsylvania on American Airlines Flight 57, in order to thwart the designs of those who sought to crash the airplane into another government building in order to inflict more pain and suffering. After asking a cell phone operator to say the "Our Father" with him, and to tell his wife Lisa that he loved her, he said the words that have now become so familiar to many Americans, "Let's Roll!"[30] He, along with others on the flight, refused to be overwhelmed by the power of evil and death, but instead became "living memorials" of courage and goodness. So, in answer to the question, "Where was God on September 11?" I believe that God was in the voice and heart and thoughts and hands of Todd Beamer.

Similarly, on that fateful day, God was in the mind and heart of Mychal Judge. A Chaplain for the New York City Fire Department, Fr. Mychal followed the firemen and women responding to the explosion in the World Trade Center Towers into the smoke and chaos that engulfed New York's tallest structures when they were struck by two passenger planes hijacked by terrorists. "For 10 years prior to September 11, he had put his own life at risk in order to provide comfort and consolation to the injured and wounded."[31] As a result of his desire to serve those he loved, he placed himself in harm's way and lost his life while discharging his priestly duties at the Twin Towers. When urged to leave the building as it began to collapse all around him he was heard to say through the smoke and the dust, "I am not finished here." Where was God on September 11? I believe that God was in the voice and heart and thoughts and hands of Fr. Mychal Judge.

And, each time that we, like the Good Samaritan, Rebecca Anderson, Cornelius Abraham, Todd Beamer, or Fr. Mychal Judge, seek to overcome evil with good, and are willing to tend to the wounds of our neighbors, in effect, God will also be in our voice, our hearts, our thoughts and our hands. And, whenever we are willing to exercise our God-given talents and gifts in order to touch and heal the wounds we encounter in this life, we will, in the words of John Paul II at Yad Vashem, "ensure that never again will evil prevail…our teachings demand that we overcome evil with good." In recalling the story of the Good Samaritan, I mentioned the misfortune of the man who was robbed, beaten and left for dead on the road to Jericho and how he was tended to and carried to safety by a man despised for his race and religion.

COMPASSION NEEDS A FACE

Some years ago, a similar story was told to the world about another man. Unfortunately, the man was not only beaten, but was abused in a way that so diminished the value of human life that it created a sense of shock and outrage all over the country. He was chained to a pickup truck and dragged to a cruel and senseless death. Apparently, the only motive for this terrible torture to be inflicted was that the victim in this story, James Bird, of Jasper, Texas, happened to be black. His abductors and murderers, three East Texas men, all by their own admission, white supremacists, are awaiting death by lethal injection in the Texas penal system.

Looking back at this vicious racial hate crime, I wonder why God did not do something about this. Possibly, the friends and family of James Bird have pondered the same question. In other words, "God, how could you let this happen?" Of course, I do not know the answer to that question. I can only wonder if anyone on that dark and winding Texas highway heard the screams of James Bird, Jr. And, although we may never know the answer, if someone did hear the cries in the night why was no help given? We may never know. But, something that we can be certain of is that during the course of our own lives, there will be moments, there will be times, when traveling along the road to Jericho we, too, will encounter the wounds and hurts of another.

Will we hear the cries of sorrow? Will we touch and cleanse the wounds and hurts of another? Will we carry him or her to a place of safety? Will we honor the human dignity of all persons we encounter? If the example of the Good Samaritan, given to us by Jesus so long ago, has anything to teach us in our own day, it is that each and every time we pour out the oil of compassion and mercy upon the wounds of our neighbor, we overcome evil with good. And, it will be through our actions on behalf of the wounded that the world will come to know the depth of our love.

At the entrance gate to the National Memorial in Oklahoma City are inscribed the words, "May all who leave here know the impact of violence. May this memorial offer comfort, strength, peace, hope and serenity." Periodically, while seated at my office desk, I look up from my work to glance at a photograph of that entrance gate that sits on my desk. Standing at the foot of the towering gate is a small elderly gentleman, cane in hand, admiring the imposing gate. That man is my 90 year old father who traveled with me to see the monument when it was first opened to the public. Over the years, I have often admired that photo of Dad standing at the gate, and it has made me smile. I suppose it helps me remember how often over the years my father has embodied the words inscribed in stone. He, too, has offered me and my brothers and sisters, comfort, strength, peace, hope, and serenity during the difficult and painful times of our own lives. In this way, he has been a "living memorial" for his own family. And when all is said and done, a "living memorial" is what Jesus calls all of us to be as we travel along the road to Jericho.

Chapter IV

Forgiveness Has a Face

Late I have learned to love you, Beauty, at once so ancient and so new! Late have I come to love you! You were within me, and I was in the world outside myself…You were with me, but I was not with you.[32]

A Parent's Love Never Wavers

On Thursday, March 13, 2003, the world awoke to the news that Elizabeth was alive. All over the country newspaper headlines announced in large bold letters: "Elizabeth Smart Found Alive," "After Nine Long Months, Utah Girl is Found," and "Miracles Do Happen, Utah Teen Found Alive." These headlines and many others like them were like the sound of a trumpet blaring glad tidings of joy. For months, the attention of much of the country had focused on the missing fourteen year old who had been abducted while sleeping in a bedroom of her parent's Salt Lake City home. Mysteriously, Elizabeth had disappeared, and despite the efforts of thousands of police and volunteers to find her, she remained lost. Experts on child abductions feared the worst. They feared that, in all likelihood, Elizabeth would never be found, and if found someday, it would be her remains, only.

But the nightmare that so many feared never came true. Instead, bad news became good news. Elizabeth was not only alive, but found by the police only a few short miles from her home in Salt Lake City. When questioned about his daughter's safe return, Ed Smart, speaking before national television cameras, said to reporters that he couldn't bear to ask his daughter about her horrible experience. On her first night home he just hugged her, told her that he loved her, and told her how happy he was to have her home.

While others had given up hope that Elizabeth could still be alive, while the police had stopped searching for her, and while others believed her to be dead, her parents had never stopped believing; they had never given up hope. Even when all seemed lost, when all seemed hopeless, Elizabeth's parents never wavered in their belief that someday their daughter would come home. Their love was enduring, their hope unending. Their daughter, who had suffered terribly at the hands of a deranged kidnapper, was now home, and their family was made whole again.

In a few simple sentences, Ed Smart, Elizabeth's father, captured the enduring and unconditional love of a parent for a child. Elizabeth was lost; now she was found. For nine months, she was feared dead; now she was alive. While others had given up searching for Elizabeth and had given up believing that she would be returned safely home, her parents kept their hope alive. Now, their sorrow had turned into joy. Now, their worst fears had been transformed into happiness. Tears of anguish had become tears of joy.

Long ago, a story was told about another parent whose love and hope were just as enduring as the love of Elizabeth's parents. Faced with the painful decision of his son to leave home of his own free will, this father waited and believed that someday his son would return safely home. The story, as first told by Jesus, was one of three stories used to describe things that were lost, but after a search were found again. The three things included a lost sheep, a lost coin, and a lost son. In each particular instance, to the delight and joy of the owner, that which was lost was found and ultimately restored to its proper place.

Jesus tells this collection of stories to illustrate God's joy upon the return of someone who has wandered far from God and for a time is seemingly lost. Just as the father of the lost son rejoices upon his son's return, so too does God in heaven feel joy and happiness when one of his children returns to God wholeheartedly. In fact, Jesus puts it this way, "...I tell you, there will be more joy in heaven over one sinner who repents than over ninety-nine respectable people who do not need to repent."[33]

A Boy and His Grandpa Take a Walk

In telling these stories about the lost son, the lost sheep, and the lost coin, Jesus wishes to teach us something about the essential nature of God. That is, that God's very "essence" is all about loving His creation. And God's "creation" is you and I. Let me put it another way. I once heard a beautiful little story, told to me by a Frenchman, to illustrate this point about God's love for His children.

A little boy and his grandfather were walking through the park one glorious sunny day. The little boy was very inquisitive, and, while they walked, would ask his grandfather some pretty interesting questions. For instance, when they came to a beautiful flowing stream that was filled with fresh blue water, the little boy would ask, "Granpapa, who made the water?" His grandfather answered, "God made the water, all the water of all the streams and all the lakes and all the oceans of the world." "Wow!" said the little boy. And when they came to a cluster of tall majestic trees that seemed to rise up to the clouds, the little boy asked, "Granpapa, who made all the trees?" His grandfather said rather matter-of-factly, "Well, God did. God made every tree, great and small, every branch, and every leaf of every shade of green and brown and orange." "Wow!" responded the little boy. This time he was even more impressed by his grandfather's response. Finally, when they came to a place in their walk where they sat by the stream under the shade of a big oak tree, the little boy wondered about all the people they had encountered on their walk. And then he asked inquisitively, "And Granpapa, who made all the people?" And again without hesitating, his grandfather told him, "Well, God did, of course! God made you and me, and everybody, of every color and every size, and every language." This time the little boy let out a giant sigh and said as before, "Wow!" And then he said, "But Granpapa, if God can make all the water, and all the trees, and all the people, too, is there anything God cannot do?" At this his grandfather told him, "Yes. There is one thing that God can not do." And looking into his grandson's eyes and gently stroking the hair on the crown of the little boy's head, the wise old man simply said, "The one thing God can never do, my little grandson, is this. God can never stop loving you."

The story illustrates a profound point about God's unconditional love. And yet, after all these years have passed, why is it that so many of us, who believe that Jesus is the perfect manifestation of God's love, have been so slow to put into practice his love and acceptance of sinners? Why is it that instead of feeling the joy that Jesus spoke about when the lost sheep returned to the flock, we have often treated those who have strayed from the church with disdain and hostility? In answer to this question, most observers would probably say that instead of feeling welcome, people who live on the margins of society feel fear or dread that they will be judged and rejected or held in scorn and contempt by those who belong to a church or religious institution. Another reason for the reluctance on the part of many people to approach the church (or people associated with religious institutions) is the betrayal of trust and loss of confidence in the very people who were supposed to be the safeguarders of religion. In recent memory, such trust, once taken for granted, has further eroded as the media has exposed scandal after scandal in the press. Such scandals have created great pain in the lives of many believers. In the face of such betrayal, how do we regain people's trust? In addition, how do we help others who have experienced a betrayal of trust in their own personal lives?

There is a moving account told in the gospels about a woman who was scorned and held in contempt by a religious authority of Jesus' day. One evening at a dinner hosted by a prominent man named Simon, she approached Jesus without fear or hesitation. She approached him with an inner serenity and peace that he would not reject her because of her sins or public reputation. Unlike the other guests, she had not been invited to the dinner but nevertheless, she began to wash the feet of Jesus with her tears and to dry his feet with her hair. This shocked the sensibilities of the invited guests who then scoffed at the woman's gesture and whispered that if Jesus were really a prophet he would know that the woman at his feet was a notorious sinner.

Sensing their moral indignation, Jesus said, "Simon, when I entered your home, you gave me no water for my feet, but she has bathed my feet with her tears and dried them with her hair. You gave me no kiss, but from the time I came in she has not stopped kissing my feet. You did not anoint my head with oil, but she has anointed my feet with an ointment. Therefore, I tell you, her sins, which were many, have been forgiven; hence she has shown great love." In spite of the moral indignation so evident in the other invited guests, Jesus then said to her, "Your sins are forgiven...Your faith has saved you; go in peace."[34]

In the final analysis, Jesus' treatment of sinners, and those whom society rejected as morally repugnant, is intended to teach us something about how we ought to treat others that the world labels as outcasts. Some years ago I happened to drive by a storefront church that had in big bold letters the following words painted on the front window, "ONLY SINNERS WELCOME HERE". At first the sign struck me as a rather bold statement. But later, it dawned on me that the members of the little storefront church have truly captured the essence of what it means to follow Jesus. After all, in his own society, Jesus would have been considered an outcast and, not by any stretch of the imagination a member of the ethical establishment or moral elite.

Indeed, even a rather superficial reading of the New Testament can quickly glean that a number of Jesus' contemporaries judged him to be outside of that which was considered to be morally correct. Consider the following statements critical of Jesus' stance toward sinners and outcasts:

"Why do you eat and drink with tax collectors and other outcasts?"[35]

"Later on Jesus was having a meal in Levi's house. A large number of tax collectors and other outcasts were following Jesus, and many of them joined him and his disciples at the table. Some teachers of the Law, who were Pharisees, saw that Jesus was eating with these outcasts and tax collectors, so they asked his disciples, 'Why does he eat with such people?'"[36]

Perhaps these criticisms, and others like them, prompted Jesus' response to his critics, "Do not judge others, and God will not judge you; do not condemn others, and God will not condemn you; forgive others, and God will forgive you…"[37] And, in even more candid and pointed terms, "I tell you: the tax collectors and the prostitutes are going into the Kingdom of God ahead of you."[38]

JESUS VISITS THE **IRS** MAN

Another memorable example of Jesus lovingly reaching out to the "lost sheep" is found in Chapter 19 of the gospel of Luke. A notorious character by the name of Zacchaeus was anxious to see Jesus as he passed through the town of Jericho. Unable to see the itinerant rabbi, because he was short in stature and his view was obstructed, Zacchaeus climbed up on the branches of a sycamore tree to catch a glimpse of Jesus.

This must have come as a real shock to those who had assembled to greet the famous teacher. But an even greater shock took place when Jesus said to this despised tax collector (long before there was an IRS, tax collectors already existed), "Hurry down, Zacchaeus, because I must stay in your house today." Upon hearing this exchange, people grumbled and said, "This man has gone as a guest to the home of a sinner!"; then moved by Jesus' unconditional acceptance, the man so notoriously a public sinner had a change of heart. He vowed to give half of his belongings to the poor and to repay those he had cheated or swindled in the exercise of his duties. When he saw his change of heart, Jesus said to Zacchaeus, "Salvation has come to this house today, for this man, also, is a descendant of Abraham. The Son of Man came to seek and to save the lost."[39]

What is really stunning about the unconditional acceptance of Zacchaeus by Jesus is that it came not after Zacchaeus had repented and made amends, but rather, it came before any external display of guilt, remorse, or reparation for his sin. Such was the love of Jesus for the lost sheep and even the most public of sinners. To put it mildly, this unconditional acceptance of Jesus for the sinner, before the sinner was restored to a state of grace by undergoing the prescribed temple ritual for the remission of sin, would be considered shocking to even the most benevolent Jewish scholar or Pharisee of first century Judaism.

ACCEPT THAT YOU ARE ACCEPTED

What was normally expected before a sinner could be fully restored to temple worship and community acceptance was a form of ritual expression for the forgiveness (or remission) of sin performed by the sinner as prescribed in the Law of Moses. That Jesus would not require the usual temple sacrifice before extending unconditional love and forgiveness to Zacchaeus is a practice unique to the character, ministry, and person of Jesus in the New Testament. In other words, Jesus' love goes out to the "lost sheep" long before the "lost sheep" is able (or even willing) to change his or her heart.

This radical form of love by Jesus for the lost sheep, and often despised members of his society, is described in some detail by Professor E.P. Sanders, widely regarded as one of the greatest authorities on the life of Jesus in the English-speaking world. In his brilliant study, *The Historical Figure of Jesus*, Sanders offers a compelling explanation for the radical love of Jesus, and why that love goes to the sinner before any requirement is made for temple sacrifice or public repentance. According to Sanders, "Jesus thought and said that the wicked who followed him, though they had not technically 'repented,' and though they had not become righteous in the way required by the law, would be in the kingdom, and in fact would be 'ahead' of those who were righteous by the law." Sanders points to this unconditional acceptance of sinners by Jesus, before he required any outward sign of repentance, as to the nature of, "just how radical Jesus was: far more radical than someone who simply committed minor infringements of the Sabbath and food laws." Hence, Jesus "seems to have thought that those who followed him belonged to God's elect, even though they did not do what the Bible itself requires."

To further illustrate Jesus' unconditional acceptance of the "lost sheep," Sanders adds, "We should recall the conclusion of one of Jesus' parables, the servants of the king, who went out into the streets and gathered all whom they found, both bad and good; so the wedding hall was filled with guests. (Mt. 22:10) The servants did not first require the bad to become good; they brought them in anyway."[40]

Thus, what can be safely deduced from this idea of the unconditional acceptance of Jesus for the sinner is that even when we look at ourselves as unlovable, unredeemable, and unworthy, Jesus continues to look at us with love. Even if we have been taught by our own particular set of circumstances that at times we are not worthy of God's love or that our flaws and imperfections make us unlovable, Jesus continues to look at us in much the same way that he looked upon the wounded and lost sheep of his own day.

He will look at us in much the same way that he looked upon the tax collector so reviled by his own neighbors, or in the same way he looked upon the woman at the home of Simon, who, in spite of her detractors, bathed his feet with her tears and dried them with her hair. It is striking to note that in another retelling of this story, Mark, the evangelist, has preserved a unique tribute paid to this woman by none other than Jesus, himself. According to some scholars of the New Testament, it is the only such tribute paid by Jesus to anyone in the entire New Testament. "Now, I assure you that wherever the gospel is preached all over the world, what she has done will be told in memory of her."[41]

The nature of God is to love his creation unconditionally, and Jesus, the perfect manifestation of God, teaches us the character of that divine love by his preferential acceptance and love of the lost and wounded sheep. I should like to retell the story of a "lost sheep" who came to discover during the course of his own life, God's unconditional love and acceptance for him. The story also illustrates, in a way similar to that of the story of Elizabeth Smart, how the enduring love of a parent mirrors the enduring love of God for those who are lost.

A Son Makes His Mother Weep

In this particular instance, the name of the "lost sheep" was Augustine. Sometimes he is referred to in devotional settings as Saint Augustine. Augustine was born in the year 354 in the town of Tagaste in North Africa. Augustine was the oldest of three sons born to a Christian mother by the name of Monica and to her husband, Patricius. While he was growing up, it became clear to his family that Augustine was a brilliant student. He was also quite independent and rather rebellious. So, at the age of 17, Augustine decided that he knew what was best for him, and against the wishes of his mother, decided to leave home in pursuit of his dreams. This was hard on his mother who wanted her son to embrace the

Christian faith. Instead, Augustine's life took some rather painful turns. He chose to embrace the teachings of a religious cult, the Manichees, who separated creation into two categories good (spirit) and evil (matter) with nothing in between. This was such a stark separation that they were branded heretics by the church. Later, Augustine would enter into a relationship with a woman that lasted fourteen years. And, although he fathered a son, he never married her. To put it mildly, this certainly went against the acceptable moral practice of the time.

At the age of twenty-nine, he announced to his mother that he was going to leave North Africa in order to become a philosophy teacher in Rome. He agreed that his mother, now a widow could travel with him, but then he suddenly left before she could follow him. Many years later in his book, *The Confessions*, he would describe this episode in his life. While his mother was weeping and praying for him, he admitted deceiving her with a lie. When Monica later traveled to Rome to try to locate Augustine, she discovered that he had never gone to Rome in the first place.

Instead, he traveled to the city of Milan. It was there that his life would begin to take a remarkable turn. In Milan he met the man who would become his future mentor and friend, the bishop of the city, Ambrose. It was Ambrose who began to explain to him the truths of the Christian faith that would ultimately lead to his conversion. Four years later, at the age of thirty-three, Augustine was baptized by Ambrose at the Easter Vigil with his mother, Monica, at his side. Having been reunited shortly before his conversion, Monica had never given up hope and had never stopped believing that one day her son would become a Christian.

Shortly after his reception into the Christian faith, Augustine began the long journey back home to North Africa. With Monica at his side, they came to the city of Ostia, when they encountered a tragedy that they could not foresee. There, so far away from home, Monica fell seriously ill and never was able to recover. With

Augustine at her bedside she reminded him that all she ever wanted was to live long enough to see him become a Catholic Christian. In later years he reflected back on the experience of losing his mother after his conversion and he readily admitted to having wept for having deceived her.

After his return to North Africa, Augustine continued his study of the faith, and four years later was pressed by the people to be ordained a priest. Then thirty-seven years old, he would remain their priest for only the next five years, when the people would press him again to become their bishop. And so he did. For the next thirty five years, until his death, he would be their bishop. He was widely known for his defense of the faith and his love for his people. Perhaps the following excerpt from one of his sermons will provide some insight as to just how far this once rebellious and impulsive young man had traveled during the course of his life: "He who is head of the people must in the first place realize that he is to be the servant of many. And he should not disdain being as such, because the Lord of Lords did not disdain to make himself our servant."

Augustine had come home. He was once lost, but in large measure because of the enduring and unwavering love of his mother, he was home again. This man who once said, "My heart is restless O God until it rests in thee," could finally find "rest." And by the grace and mercy of God, he could be "restored" by God to a place of greater dignity and self-worth. Like his mother, Monica, God never gave up on Augustine. And, in spite of his wounds, his disappointments, his failures, and his imperfections, God continued to love him, completely and unconditionally.

In spite of our own imperfections and failures, God will continue to love you and me. This is the very heart and core of the message and life of Jesus. This is the very essence of God. Jesus spent his whole life and ministry trying to teach us this very important lesson. How very different the world would be if only we put this "core" of Jesus' message into practice. Perhaps we would begin to see that we are lovable, and that others, in spite of their own particular flaws, are lovable, too.

THE WOUND THAT LETS GOD IN

In this regard, I find the works of Rabbi Harold Kushner to be very helpful. Writing from the perspective of the Jewish faith and Hebrew Scriptures, Rabbi Kushner argues that in its finest hour, religion and spirituality should help to welcome the sinner in his or her state of imperfection. In his book, *How Good Do We Have to Be? A New Understanding of Guilt and Forgiveness,* Kushner explains, "Yes, religion can make us feel guilty by setting standards for us, holding up ideals against which we can measure ourselves. But that same religion can then welcome us in our imperfection. It can comfort us with the message that God prefers the broken and contrite heart that knows its failures over the complacent and arrogant one that claims never to have erred."[42]

Kushner also makes an important distinction between the role of priest and prophet in the Bible. In the history of Israel the prophet was the one called by God to challenge and chastise the sinner, while the priest was sent by God to restore the sinner back into the good graces of God and the community. In Kushner's own words: "The prophet chastised sinners, the priest welcomed them to the altar. We need both as ancient Israel needed both. We need the demanding voice of the prophet to hold us to high standards, so that we can grow and be all that we are capable of being…And we need the comforting voice of the priest to assure us that even when we don't feel we deserve to be loved, God loves us anyway because He is a loving and forgiving God who knows us too well to expect more from us than we are capable of being."[43]

Another way of seeing how God truly loves us in spite of our imperfections is articulated by Ernest Kurtz and Katherine Ketcham in their 1992 book, *The Spirituality of Imperfection.* Employing the imagery of imperfection as a "wound," the authors say, "God comes through the wound. Our imperfections–what religion labels our 'sins,' what therapy calls our 'sickness,' what philosophy terms our 'errors,'–are precisely what bring us closer to the reality that no matter how hard we try to deny it, we are not the ones in control here. And this realization, inevitably and joyously, brings us closer to God."[44]

To drive home their point of God using the wounds of our imperfections in order to draw nearer to us, Kurtz and Ketcham include a retelling of a story by Anthony De Mello: "One of the disconcerting—and delightful—teachings of the master was: 'God is closer to sinners than to saints.' This is how he explained it: 'God in heaven holds each person by a string. When you sin, you cut the string. Then God ties it up again, making a knot -and thereby brings you a little closer to Him. Again and again your sins cut the string-and with each further knot God keeps drawing you closer and closer."[45]

The essential nature of God is an unconditional love for all of His creation. And His "creation" is you and I. Like the enduring love of a parent who continues to search for a lost son or lost daughter until he or she is returned safely home, Jesus teaches us, in his life and ministry, that God continues to love us in spite of our flaws and imperfections. As the grandfather responded to his little grandson, "The one thing God cannot do, is that God can never stop loving you!"

If we truly embrace the idea that God continues to love us, even when we fail, even when we disappoint Him, even in spite of all of our imperfections, then we will begin to understand the depth of God's unconditional love. In the words of one New Testament writer: "This is what love is: it is not that we have loved God, but that he loved us and sent his Son to be the means by which our sins are forgiven."[46]

I'M THE GREATEST HITTER IN THE WORLD

A funny little story is told about a boy who was alone in his backyard playing baseball. "I'm the greatest hitter in the world!" he would say as he tossed the ball in the air, swung hard, and missed. "Strike one!" he yelled. He picked up the ball and said again, "I'm the greatest hitter in the world!" This time, feeling more confident, he tossed up the ball, and swung, and missed. "Strike two!" The boy then examined his bat and his ball. He spit on his hands, rubbed them together, tugged his cap and repeated, "I'm the greatest hitter in the world!" Again he tossed up the ball, swung mightily, and missed. "Strike three!" Then the little boy exclaimed, "I'm the greatest pitcher in the world!"

While we may not be the world's greatest hitter, pitcher, singer or painter, in the eyes of God, and in the eyes of Jesus, we are worthy to be loved and worthy to be saved and forgiven. Sometimes in our own lives, like Elizabeth Smart, like Augustine of Tagaste, like Zacchaeus the tax collector or like the woman who wept at Jesus' feet, we will feel like the sheep that has gone astray. If we are fortunate to live long enough, in time we will make our share of mistakes, and perhaps some of those personal failures will make us feel far away from God.

Throughout the span of over twenty years of ministry I have often listened to the stories of men and women who have shared openly their personal experiences of sin and brokenness. Sometimes the conversations have taken place in formal settings, such as an office or confessional. Other times, these conversations have been in informal surroundings such as an airport lounge, in between innings of a baseball game, during backyard barbeques, or while sharing a meal at a restaurant. Regardless of how formal or informal the setting may be, often I say to the person sharing his or her struggles or disappointments, that in my years in the priesthood I have come to understand two things of which we can be certain of. The first is that there is a God. The second is that it is not me and it is not you. Therefore, we can only trust that it is God, and God alone, who will forgive our failings and our sins. And then, I will often ask them to read with me the words of Psalm 51, or I will recite some of the verses from memory.

> Be Merciful to me, O God, because of your constant love. Because of your great mercy wipe away all my sins! Wash away all my evil and make me clean from my sin…I have sinned against you—only against you—and done what you consider evil…Remove my sin, and I will be clean; wash me, and I will be whiter than snow…Close your eyes to my sins and wipe out all my evil. Create a pure heart in me, O God, and put a new and loyal spirit in me…My sacrifice is a humble spirit, O God; you will not reject a humble and repentant heart.[47]

If there is one other thing we can be certain of, from the way that Jesus loved the lost sheep of his own day, it is that God is always ready and willing to carry us in his loving and forgiving arms. Love consists in this: not that we have first loved God, but that God has first loved us. This assurance was given to the people of Israel from the beginning of their history, as God's personal pledge and promise to His chosen people. It is a promise that became embodied in the person and life of Jesus of Nazareth, the human face of God.

TONY SOPRANO, THE AMISH,
AND TODAY YOU WILL BE WITH ME IN PARADISE.

Some years ago cable television created a weekly television series about the life of a fictional New Jersey crime boss. If you have ever watched an episode of the *Sopranos* you know that Tony Soprano, the lead character, spends a considerable amount of time in therapy. With the help of Dr. Melphi, his "shrink," he repeatedly tries to seek absolution for his terrible misdeeds. However, each time Dr. Melphi tries to point out his bad behavior, Tony Soprano only rationalizes his actions and continues to seek out vengeance on those who try to cross him. No amount of rationalizing or trying to buy the affections of those he wounds will ever give Tony Soprano the feeling of forgiveness for which he longs. Instead, each act of vengeance and violence only serves to do more violence to his soul already diminished by betrayal and self-deception.

Although forgiveness may be elusive for the character of Tony Soprano, it is not elusive for those of us who open our hearts to God with humility and contrition. Indeed, we have only to place before God our failings and transgressions, while at the same time we must be willing to forgive the failings and transgressions of others. To paraphrase the words of the late, great, John Paul II, "an act of merciful love is only truly such when we are convinced that at the same time that we *give forgiveness,* we are *receiving forgiveness* from those who are accepting it from us. To put it another way, forgiveness is often a two way street.

In the fall of 2006 a deranged gunman walked into a rural Pennsylvania school house and took ten children hostage. The children, all girls ranging in age from seven to thirteen belonged to a tightly knit group of orthodox Christians known as the Amish. When confronted by local law enforcement the gunman turned the gun on the children immediately killing five of the girls before taking his own life. In the aftermath of this terrible crime, friends and acquaintances of the gunman wondered what could have motivated the thirty-two year old former milkman to do something so heinous. The only clue that pointed to any motive was a letter addressed to his wife describing his anger toward God.

In the days following the terrible events of the shooting a small newspaper story recounting the details of the funeral of the killer caught my eye. About seventy-five mourners gathered in a small Methodist church to pay their respects to the family of Charles Roberts, the gunman. What was striking, indeed remarkable to me was that of the seventy-five mourners in attendance approximately half were from the Amish community. In spite of the terrible and tragic events that had befallen them, in spite of the great harm done to them by Charles Roberts, their presence underscored their unshakable faith in God and humanity. Indeed it was noted by more than one mourner that the example of unconditional love and forgiveness offered by the Amish to the wife of the man who had done them so much harm simply made them break down in tears.

The example of this simple, yet noble, group of farmers has something to teach all of us. We long to experience forgiveness in our own lives, and oftentimes, we wish we were more capable of forgiving those who harm us. And yet, often we carry grudges for the most ridiculous slight or snubs (or perceived snubs) and we say to ourselves, if not to others, "hell will freeze over before I forgive that person!" If we need in our own lives a greater impetus or desire to forgive others, indeed to forgive ourselves, then the Amish truly give forgiveness a human face for us to ponder. That face is not unlike the face of another who long ago on a hillside overlooking Jerusalem, spoke to a common criminal who pleaded with him, "Jesus, remember me when you come into your kingdom." Jesus, himself, the victim of a terrible injustice, spoke in loving words to him who pleaded so, "Today you will be with me in paradise."

Chapter V

Courage Has a Face

Forgiveness was definitely within the Jewish tradition of Jesus, but many conditions had to be fulfilled before forgiveness could be granted. In many ways, the offended seems to be the ultimate judge of whether forgiveness was deserved or not. This could easily lead to a form of revenge and righteous punishment. Jesus goes much further by placing the root of forgiveness not in the one offended, but in the very heart of God, our merciful parent.[48]

ON THE EDGE OF MADNESS

In the early part of April, 1985, Terry Anderson asked his captors for a Bible. For twenty-four days he had been chained to a wall by his wrists and forced to lie on a steel frame cot for hours at a time, his face covered with a blindfold. Not knowing from one moment to the next if he would live or die, he was, as he put it, "on the edge of madness." On March 16 Terry had been kidnapped by Islamic militants while covering the war in West Beirut, Lebanon as a correspondent for the Associated Press. Since the day of his capture Terry had been kept in total isolation with the exception of the daily interruptions for feeding and being led in chains to the toilet. Completely despondent, humiliated, and hopeless, Terry not only feared for his own life, but for the safety and well being of his pregnant wife, Madeleine.

By his own admission, Terry had never been a particularly religious person. For years he had not practiced the faith of his childhood and youth, Catholicism. Now, in almost total desperation, fear permeating virtually every fiber of his body, he had pleaded for his captors to bring him a Bible. Removing the blindfold from his eyes, Terry looked down to read the words in front of him, "In the Beginning." Little could Terry have known that those first twenty-four days in isolation were going to stretch into the longest seven years of his life.

For those seven long years, while being subjected to terrible indignities and every sort of human depravity, Terry Anderson clung to his Bible. Often alone, sometimes held in captivity with other hostages, Terry clung to his Bible. Throughout his terrible and sometimes excruciating ordeal, Terry would come to find in the pages of his Bible the strength and courage to overcome the torments of his captors. Throughout the long periods of anger, illness, disease, frustration, hopelessness, doubt and the seemingly endless dashed hopes when freedom would never come, Terry persevered in his faith. And, while everything around him seemed utterly hopeless, Terry continued to summon the gifts of faith and courage within him.

I believe the ordeal suffered by Terry Anderson at the hands of the Islamic Jihad has much to teach us about the gifts of faith and courage. Perhaps none of us will ever have to suffer the horrible fate of being kept in solitary confinement, torn away from those we love, subjected to beatings and mock executions, to scorn and humiliation; yet the story of Terry Anderson teaches us to keep the faith even in the face of the greatest trials and tribulations life has to offer. It is a story that says, even when things go wrong, even when darkness comes, even when there seems to be no reason to keep believing, that we must never give up. In the case of Terry Anderson he mustered the strength and intestinal fortitude to say deep within himself, "Even in the face of death, even in the face of despair, evil will not win. Although my captors ridicule me, although my enemies revile me, God is with me and I will prevail!"

Throughout his captivity Terry found added strength from his reading of the Psalms of the Hebrew Bible. While many of them spoke directly to him throughout his situation of being held hostage, one of the psalms in particular seems to apply to many of us, who like Terry, at some point in our lives will have to come face to face with evil, suffering, and disappointment. The psalm, one of the most treasured of all the psalms, says:

> The Lord is my shepherd; I have everything I need. He lets me rest in fields of green grass and leads me to quiet pools of fresh water. He gives me new strength. He guides me in right paths, as he has promised. Even if I go through the deepest darkness, I will not be afraid, Lord, for you are with me. Your shepherd's rod and staff protect me. You prepare a banquet for me, where all my enemies can see me; you welcome me as an honored guest and fill my cup to the brim. I know that your goodness and love will be with me all my life; and your house will be my home as long as I live.[49]

During his seven long years as a hostage Terry Anderson walked through the darkest valley imaginable and perhaps that dark valley is reflected in his thoughts as he approached his second birthday in captivity. In the journal of his years in captivity, Anderson describes his struggle to keep his faith and hope alive. Although he tried praying, sometimes for hours, his despair would inevitably overwhelm him. Thus, frustration, anger, bitterness and disgust would come like waves of water pouring over him.

At certain times during his imprisonment, Terry felt that God had abandoned him, and wondered why God would put him through such pain and humiliation. But, despite his fears, anger, frustration and loneliness, Terry trusted that the God of the Twenty- Third Psalm was with him as he walked through the valley of darkness and shame. In time, because of his faith and courage, because of the unconditional love of his family, who lobbied countless government officials for his release, and because of the support he received from other hostages, Terry was able to survive and come to a deeper and more meaningful relationship with God. Once granted his freedom, he was able to truly say that God had set a banquet before him in the sight of his enemies and that the good shepherd of Psalm 23 had walked by his side through the deepest darkness imaginable.

THE MOST FREQUENT COMMAND IN THE BIBLE

During his captivity the words of Psalm 23, "I will not be afraid, Lord, for you are with me. Your shepherd's rod and staff protect me," truly spoke to Terry and gave him strength and hope. These powerful words and images also speak to the hearts of many believers who, like Terry Anderson, need God's comfort and consolation in times of trouble and anxiety. Perhaps it is no accident that the Bible spends a considerable amount of time dealing with the subject of fear. Consider the words of N. T. Wright, a scholar of the New Testament, on the subject of fear in the Bible.

> Do you know what the most frequent command in the Bible turns out to be? What instruction, what order, is given, again and again, by God, by angels, by Jesus, by prophets and apostles? What do you think -'Be good'? 'Be holy, for I am holy'? Or negatively, 'Don't sin'? 'Don't be immoral'? No. The most frequent command in the Bible is: *Don't be afraid.* 'Don't *be afraid. Fear not. Don't be afraid.*"... This surprising command bursts in upon a world in which we eat, sleep, and breathe fear. We emerge from the warmth of the womb into the cold of the cosmos, and we're afraid of being alone, of being unloved, of

being abandoned. We mix with other children, other teen-agers, other young adults, and we're afraid of looking stupid, of being left behind in some race that we all seem to be automatically entered for. We contemplate jobs, and we're afraid both that we mightn't get the one we really want and that if we get it we mightn't be able to do it properly; and that double fear lasts for many people all through their lives. We contemplate marriage, and we're afraid both that we might never find the right person and that if we do marry it may turn out to be a disaster. We consider a career move, and are afraid both of stepping off the ladder and of missing the golden opportunity. We look ahead to retirement, and are afraid both of growing older and more feeble and of dying suddenly. Let's make no mistake about it: until you learn to live without fear you won't find it easy to follow Jesus.[50]

N. T. Wright describes the all too common condition and feeling shared by many of us who seek to pattern our own lives after Jesus. The feeling is best described as the lifelong struggle to overcome the fears in our lives so that we might live in freedom as sons and daughters of God. To live in fear is to be paralyzed by the circumstances, people, or events around us. To live in fear is to carry around our necks the "albatross" that is dread, worry, and anxiety, simply because we can never be precisely sure how certain things or problems in our lives will work out. To live in fear is to be weighed down by the situations where we have very little control, instead of simply trusting the Author of Life for the outcome of those uncertain situations.

And yet, fear, although very much a part of everyday life is precisely what Jesus came to help us transform and dispel by his own life and ministry. Actually, it seems that throughout the course of his life Jesus spent a considerable amount of time and energy helping others overcome the paralysis of fear. Consider the words spoken by the angel Gabriel to Mary the Mother of Jesus, announcing his birth at the beginning of Luke's gospel, "Don't be afraid, Mary; God has been gracious to you."[51] And then at the time of his birth, consider the words spoken by the angel to the shepherds who cared for their flocks by night, "Don't be afraid! I am here with good news for you, which will bring great joy to all the people. This very day in David's town your savior was born—Christ the Lord!"[52]

WE'RE ALL IN THE SAME BOAT

Perhaps no two experiences in the lives of the disciples better illustrate how Jesus teaches them the necessity of overcoming their fears than the following stories. Both incidents are recorded by Mark, the author of the first and most primitive gospel. In the first example Jesus and the disciples are out at sea when a violent storm erupts and causes their boat to be tossed by waves. The storm was so violent that after the episode Jesus poses the question to the disciples, "Why are you frightened? Do you still have no faith?" While the disciples feared they would be killed, Jesus was sound asleep in the stern and once awakened by the disciples said to the storm, "Be quiet! Be still!"[53] At once the wind ceased and the storm was calm.

In a second story, while the disciples were out far from shore, their boat was tossed by the waves as they tried rowing back to safety. Suddenly, Jesus drew near to them by walking on the water. The disciples were terrified and thought that they were seeing a ghost, but at once Jesus spoke to them saying, "Courage! It is I. Don't be afraid!"[54] Afterwards, Jesus got into the boat with them and the wind subsided. At this turn of events, the disciples were rendered speechless and stood in awe of Jesus' power over the elements. It is certainly worth pointing out that while Jesus remained at a distance from the disciples they experienced fear and turbulence; it was only when Jesus drew near to them and got into the boat that their fear diminished and the winds and storm receded.

For the very earliest believers this episode amplified a truth and conviction about Jesus. When they experienced that the Lord was far away from them, they could expect the storms of life to create terror and turbulence, but when they experienced the presence of Jesus in their midst, then the storms did not overwhelm them, and neither did their fears. For the earliest believers, having Jesus in the same boat was the great source of courage and calm even in the face of the inevitable storms that they would have to encounter. The opposite was also true; without the presence of the Lord in their lives, the fears would remain and perhaps overwhelm even the strongest believer among them.

It is also important to note that in relating the story of the calming of the storm, Mark, the gospel writer, implies a direct connection to the power of Jesus over the power of evil. For instance, when Jesus calms the ferocity of the storm, he employs the expression, *"Quiet! Be still!"* Similarly, in the very first miracle story recorded by Mark, Jesus says to a man possessed by a demon in the synagogue, *Quiet! Come out of him!* In this way, Mark underscores that not only does Jesus have power over the turbulent sea, but he also has power over the manifestation of evil. As has been previously pointed out by New Testament scholars, the expression in Greek that Jesus employs to calm the sea is the same command that he uses to silence the demon in the man possessed.

A giant in the world of New Testament studies, Fr. Raymond Brown, has reinforced this connection between the calming of the sea and the expulsion of the demon in Mark's Gospel:

> Just as sickness and affliction reflect the kingdom of evil, so also does a dangerous storm; accordingly Jesus rebukes the wind and the sea in 4:39 just as he does a demon in 1:25. Lest one think this picture impossibly naive, one should note that when a storm causes death and destruction today, people wonder why God has allowed this: they do not vent their anger on a high pressure system. The victory of Jesus over the storm is seen as the action of the stronger one whom even the wind and the sea obeys.[55]

AGAINST ALL ODDS

While in biblical times the disciples looked to Jesus for courage, in modem times people often look for examples of courage and bravery in history books or movies. Recently, the former Mayor of New York City, Rudy Giuliani, credited the example of Winston Churchill during World War II for providing him an example of courage during the darkest days of his life as mayor following the attacks of September 11. Drawing inspiration from the lives of great political leaders can provide courage and inspiration when one is faced with times of struggle. For instance, during his time as Prime Minister of Great Britain at the height of the Second World War, Churchill rallied an entire nation in order to withstand and resist the German invasion of his homeland. Because of his bravery in the face of great peril, his countrymen still revere and admire him. No stranger to failure during his long political life, Churchill once remarked, "Success is going from failure to failure without loss of enthusiasm."[56]

Another great profile in courage is the sixteenth President of the United States, Abraham Lincoln. He is probably the most loved and admired president, among all of the presidents in American history. His courageous and benevolent leadership during the American Civil War, led Lincoln to say, "The probability that you may fall in the struggle ought not to deter you from the support of a cause you believe to be just."[57] Indeed, he often went against the conventional wisdom of the day knowing that he would be the object of attacks and criticism from many of his detractors. Nevertheless, he was known for his courage when it came to sticking to his principles during the worst of times.

Still, others find that the portrayal of courageous characters in literature and movies also provides inspiration and hope. In the movie *Rocky*, the actor Sylvester Stallone, portrays a fictitious boxer whose prime has passed him by, only to be given a chance to fight for the heavyweight championship of the world. Against all odds Rocky summons the personal courage to give the reigning champion the fight of his life. In the end, he makes believers out of all those who doubted his resolve and tenacity.

Similarly, in the movie, *Rudy*, Rudy Rudiger must overcome tremendous obstacles in order to succeed and prevail against overwhelming odds. Based upon the true story of a young man from the Midwest, Rudy is told that he is not big enough, or smart enough, or good enough to play football at the University of Notre Dame. Yet, despite the advice of his detractors, he spends countless hours working, studying, practicing and praying, just to become a member of the varsity practice squad. In time, not only does he succeed in becoming a member of the team, but he goes on to graduate from one of the top universities in the country. In the end, pursuing his dream was not a complete waste of time as some said, because Rudy never wavered in his courage, faith, and belief.

A SHEPHERD WALKS THE WALK

While historical figures and portrayals from the movies can inspire and motivate us to be more courageous in our personal lives, I believe that the greatest example of courage available to us can be found in the gospel of John. This example of courage is the good shepherd, who is none other than Jesus himself. Beginning in Chapter 10, John describes the qualities of this good shepherd. The good shepherd is one who is willing to lay down his life for his flock while in contrast the shepherd who works for pay abandons the flock to the wolves if he feels his own life is in danger. The good shepherd is a benevolent master of the flock who knows each sheep by name. So intimate is his knowledge of the flock, that the sheep know the sound of his voice, and respond to his commands. In contrast, the sheep will scatter when they hear the sound of the stranger's voice. Therefore, it is no accident that Jesus employs the image of the shepherd from first century Palestine in order to illustrate the depth of his love for his disciples, as well as his unwavering courage in laying down his own life for those who are members of his flock.

One writer describes the qualities of the shepherd this way:

> A real shepherd was born to his task. He was sent out with the flock as soon as he was old enough to go; the sheep became his friends and companions; and it became second nature to think of them before he thought of himself...His life was very hard. His staff was the weapon with which he defended himself and his flock against marauding beasts and robbers. In Palestine the shepherd went in front and the sheep followed. The shepherd went first to see that the path was safe, and sometimes the sheep had to be encouraged to follow. The shepherd's task was not only constant but dangerous, for in addition, he had to guard the flock against wild animals...and robbers ready to steal the sheep. Isaiah speaks of the crowd of shepherds being called out to deal with the lion (Isaiah 31:4). To the shepherd it was the most natural thing to risk his life in defense of his flock. Constant vigilance, fearless courage, patient love for his flock, were the necessary characteristics of the shepherd.[58]

This excellent description of the shepherds of Jesus' day makes it easy to see why Jesus adopts the image of the shepherd. In order to speak of the depth of his love for the members of his flock, the image communicated to his earliest listeners and disciples that he, like the shepherds of the countryside of Israel, was willing to give his own life in order to protect and rescue the sheep of his flock. Indeed one might argue that in the Gospel of John, not only is Jesus seen as the good shepherd who lays down his life for his flock, but he is also portrayed as the "Lamb of God who takes away the sin of the world."[59] Thus, in John, not only is Jesus the shepherd and head of the flock, but the sacrificial lamb as well, willing to give his life so that others may live.

Ultimately, the image of Jesus as the good shepherd is intended to teach us some very important lessons about Jesus as he is portrayed by the authors of the New Testament. In the first place, as we look at Jesus in the Gospels, we can be sure that when we walk through the darkest valleys life has to offer, Jesus will be at our side with his rod and staff to give us courage. Thus, along with Terry Anderson, along with the disciples in their tempest tossed boat, we should fear no evil for God is with us. In the person of Jesus, the Shepherd, God says to us, even in the throes of despair, depression, deep anxiety, and fear, the Shepherd is always willing to keep loving you with a love that says, "Do not be afraid. You will never be alone. I will lay down my life for you. My rod and staff will give you courage and strength." Similarly, just as the image of Jesus, the good shepherd is intended to give us strength and courage as we walk through life's darkest valleys, so, too, is the image intended to motivate us to call upon and summon the shepherd that lies within each of us.

It is rather easy to spot the good shepherd within us at work. For example, each and every time that we act upon our instincts to lay down our own lives for another person who is lonely, depressed, or fearful, the shepherd within us is at work. Each and every time that we summon the courage to stand up in defense of the poor, the abused, the oppressed, the shepherd within us is at work. And, each and every time that we walk alongside another person who is suffering from the darkness of cancer, Alzheimer's, or another terminal illness, the shepherd within us is at work. Here is one version of the 23rd Psalm as one author sees the shepherd at work in the person of the mother dedicated to her family.

THE 23RD PSALM FOR MOTHERS

My mom is my shepherd; I shall not want.
She makes me lie down under cool, downy comforts.
She watches me play beside still waters.
She restores my soul.

She leads me in paths of respect, responsibility, and goodness,
    for I am her namesake!
Yea, even though I walk past monsters in the dark,
I will not be scared, because my mom is always near me.
Her hands and her voice, they comfort me.
Mama sets the table and cheerfully calls me to dinner even in
    front of big, mean bullies.
She anoints my skinned knees and broken heart with kisses.
She smiles and throws me a towel when my cup runneth over.
Surely God's peace, power, and mercy shall uphold me all the
    days of my life, for my Mother taught me to dwell in the
    house of God forever.[60]

Walking Through the Valley Of Darkness

One who walks alongside others as they travel through the valley of darkness and death is Sister Helen Prejean. As a good shepherd, Sister Helen describes in detail the experience of walking with the condemned as they face execution by electric chair in her moving and gut-wrenching account, *Dead Man Walking*. I once asked Sister Helen why the producers of *Dead Man Walking*, the movie based on her book, elected to portray the execution scene in the movie as execution by lethal injection, instead of execution by electric chair. Her answer surprised me. Evidently by depicting the more "humane" execution by injection, the movie creators hoped to make the execution of the character portrayed by Sean Penn less offensive to the sensibilities of movie goers. Be that as it may, Sister Helen's description of the actual execution as it unfolds in the death chamber of the Louisiana State Prison is riveting. She writes about the day she accompanied the accused man, Patrick Sonnier, to the death chamber.

> I walk with Pat...I am standing behind him. Guards, a mountain of blue, surround us. I put my hand on his shoulder...It is the first time I have ever touched him. We walk. Pat walks and the

chains scrape across the floor…I read Isaiah's words: 'Do not be afraid…I have called you by your name, you are mine.'[61]

Once the guards begin to strap Patrick to the electric chair, Sister Helen is taken to the room with the glass partition that separates the witnesses from the dark oak chair where the condemned man is seated. Before the warden begins to carry out the sentence, Patrick remembers Sister Helen's instructions, "Look at my face." In a moment, a greenish gray cloth will cover his head and he will no longer see her. But for an instant Patrick finds her face. He mouths the words, "I love you." She stretches out her hand toward him and says, "I love you, too." Soon the warden nods his head in the direction of the executioner. And, as more than 4,000 volts run through his body, Sister Helen whispers, "Christ, be with him, have mercy on him."[62]

Patrick Sonnier was executed by the State of Louisiana for the murder of two teen-agers, Loretta Bourque and David LeBlanc. And yet, despite the terrible nature of his crimes, God sent Patrick Sonnier a shepherd in the person of Sister Helen Prejean. As he walked from death row to the death chamber, Helen Prejean spoke to him the same words spoken by Isaiah the Prophet, "Do not be afraid, I am with you." Some would argue that because of his guilt he did not deserve or merit the love and care of a shepherd. Some would argue that, in the end, Patrick Sonnier got what he truly deserved. But the God of Jesus sent him a shepherd, anyway. He looked through the glass partition for a kind and loving face and saw the face of the shepherd. In that face he saw courage; he saw forgiveness; he saw love. Over the years, I have often stood over the beds of the terminally ill and dying. Some young, some elderly, some able to speak, some completely motionless, some in pain, some peaceful. Often, as I gaze into their eyes, as I stroke their hair, as I anoint their forehead with oil for the sick, I wonder what they will see in my face. And then, I often think that if God allows me the grace to live a long life, the day will come when I, too, will gaze up at the face of my own shepherd. This will be true for all of us, provided God extends to us the blessing of a long life. But when it is time for us to part from this life to the next, whose face will we see? Who will be the shepherd for us? Who will gaze into our eyes? Maybe, if we are fortunate, it will be a spouse, a child, a caregiver, a brother, a sister, or a friend. But, regardless of who happens to be at our side, at the time of our own parting, I hope we will be fortunate enough to have someone who loves us with the unconditional love of the "Good Shepherd." Perhaps then they will say to us as we journey through the valley of darkness and death, "Just look at my face. Do not be afraid, I am with you! I love you. Go in peace!"

Chapter VI

Hope Has a Face

A Man of Faith Known Simply As Joe

In a column that appeared in the fall of 1996, advice columnist Ann Landers wrote about her friend, the late Cardinal Bernardin, Archbishop of Chicago. In a column entitled "A Man of Faith Known Simply as Joe," she told her readers that just prior to his death she had prayed at his bedside, and now upon receiving news of his passing was writing with a very heavy heart. She recalled that even though the Cardinal had ascended to the heights of leadership in the church, he had always considered himself just a priest, performing the everyday unglamorous tasks that he signed on for at the beginning.

> He visited the sick, quietly, anonymously, and showed up unannounced and unexpected at the bedside of cancer victims. He spoke of death as a friend and somehow made us all less afraid to die. The cardinal visited his mother in her nursing home near his residence every day without fail until he became bedridden. She would always ask him, 'What are you doing now, Joseph?' And he would reply, 'I'm working for the church, Mother.' She would say, 'That is lovely. Keep it up.' He never told her he

was a cardinal. She had no idea. Joe taught us how to live and he taught us how to die. Dear God, please take good care of this remarkable man. The likes of him will not soon pass this way again.[63]

In her tribute to Cardinal Bernardin, Ann Landers captures a quality of the man that thousands of Chicagoans, Catholics and non-Catholics alike, came to appreciate during his fourteen years as archbishop. In spite of his own personal suffering, Joseph Bernardin continued to be a person of hope. It was hope that sustained him in his battle with cancer and it was hope that others saw in him throughout the course of his life.

Three years prior to his death, this hope had given him the means to live through the terrible ordeal of having been falsely accused of sexual abuse by a young man angry at God and the church. When the young man, a former seminarian and AIDS patient, alleged that the cardinal had sexually abused him in 1975, the news of the accusation made the front page of every major newspaper in the country. Nevertheless, it was a strong hope that God would not abandon him that led Cardinal Bernardin to go before the national media to proclaim his innocence and deny the false accusation. Later on it was hope that enabled him to meet with his accuser, Steven Cook, forgive him and restore him to the sacraments of the Church.

In his own words the Cardinal spoke about his meeting with Steven Cook where the reconciliation between the two of them took place. He recalled the young man's words to him:

> …"I'm not sure I want to have Mass," he said haltingly; "I've felt very alienated from God and the church a long time."…

> …"Steven," I said, "I have brought you something, a Bible that I have inscribed to you. But I do understand, and I won't be offended if you don't want to accept it." Steven took the Bible in quivering hands, pressed it to his heart as tears welled up in his eyes…

Before Steven left, he told me, "A big burden has been lifted from me today. I feel healed and very much at peace."...

Steven and I kept in touch after that and, six months later, when I received a diagnosis of pancreatic cancer, his was one of the first letters I received. He had only a few months to live when he wrote it, filled with sympathy and encouragement for me. He planned to visit me in Chicago at the end of August, but he was too ill. Steven died at his mother's home on September 22, 1995, fully reconciled with the church. "This", he said smiling from his deathbed at his mother about his return to the sacraments, "is my gift to you." The priest in Cincinnati who attended him told this to me soon afterwards.[64]

A man of faith, known simply as Joe, had become the face of hope for a young man who had become hopeless. Steven Cook, angry, alienated and afraid saw in the face of Joseph Bernardin the face of hope. And that face of hope allowed him to ask for forgiveness from Cardinal Bernardin for having falsely accused him. In the span of three short years Cardinal Bernardin was subjected to the ordeal of being falsely accused of sexual abuse and then was told by his doctor that he had terminal cancer. His experience of suffering during this time: the humiliation suffered at the hands of his accusers, his reputation tarnished by the media, and the physical pain of pancreatic cancer could have led to depression and despair. At the very least he could have chosen, understandably, to become angry or embittered by his circumstances. Instead, Joseph Bernardin chose to become a person of hope. And to become a messenger of hope is what each of us is called to be in spite of our own failures, betrayals, and disappointments. Of course, to become that messenger of hope in the face of such obstacles is far easier said than done. To be hopeful in times of success, personal triumph, happiness, and celebration is one thing, but to be hopeful in poverty, loss, humiliation, and sorrow is quite another.

A Messenger of Hope Inspires

I once was privileged to meet one of the great, spiritual writers of the modern age, Father Henri Nouwen. Father Nouwen, now deceased, inspired many of his readers to be people of hope. Even a casual reading of any of his books on spirituality allows his readers to feel more hopeful about the most trying of circumstances. I once heard Nouwen describe what it was like to care for the severely mentally challenged in a home for the disabled. It stuck me as remarkable that someone so brilliant and intellectually gifted could exude such hope and joy when describing the simple acts of kindness extended to those who could hardly speak. Nouwen not only wrote about hope, he gave hope to those often considered hopeless.

I like to think of two distinguishing characteristics that messengers of hope share in common. The first is *messengers of hope look beyond the present moment.* Secondly, *messengers of hope maintain a healthy sense of perspective.* To look beyond the present moment is the capacity to refuse to languish in the struggles, disappointments, setbacks, and failures of daily life as if they will last forever. Rather, a messenger of hope looks beyond the present moment to a brighter day to come.

Over the years I have had to look into the eyes and faces of many mourners who grieve the loss of a loved one. Sometimes the losses are profound and tragic, as in the case of a three month old baby who died unexpectedly in the middle of the night, or the young couple who perished in a car accident traveling to their honeymoon just a few days after I presided at their wedding or two brothers and their cousin, members of a young band of musicians, whose bodies were badly burned when they lost control of their car on a rainy night.

Most of the time in speaking to those who experience such painful losses I have often been inspired by the capacity of those who experience such grief to look beyond the pain of the present moment to a brighter day to come. While the pain and sorrow of such a dramatic and sudden loss can overwhelm even the strongest believer, messengers of hope seem to possess a distinguishing characteristic that gives them the courage and the strength to move forward with the assurance that things will get better. On the other hand, those who live without a sense of hope, almost immediately see the sufferings in their lives as an eternal punishment or even abandonment by God. Other times, they utter to those around them the words of the children's fairy tale spoken by the little chicken who cried, "The sky is falling! The sky is falling!"

GOD WILL TURN OUR MOURNING INTO MORNING

As I have witnessed the remarkable courage, faith and perseverance of people, who in spite of their loss or disappointment continue to hold tight to their beliefs in goodness and hope, I often think of a powerful expression that says *God will turn our mourning into morning.* That is, God will transform the darkest gloomiest moments of our lives into something beautiful for us and others. This transformation from pain to hope may take time. But, for those who continue to hope beyond the sorrow of the present moment, the transformation will come without fail.

Imagine a ship out at sea on a cold, rainy, gloomy night trying to find its way to shore. The clouds and fog make it impossible for the captain and crew to find their way through the choppy waves. At the moment all seems lost, terrifying and hopeless. And then, out of the density of the fog and despair of the rainy night comes a light peering through the darkness and gloom. The light sits on a hilltop near the shoreline and its source is a lighthouse for all the world to see. That is the feeling one experiences when at the moments of our deepest, darkest gloom and despair, God's transformative power *turns our mourning into morning.* At that particular moment, what seems so overwhelming, even terrifying, gives way to a light that dispels darkness and allows us to find our way back to the harbor of peace and tranquility. But, this transformative experience is only possible for the messenger of hope who continues to look beyond the pain of the present moment to the promise of a brighter day that lies ahead.

A second distinguishing characteristic shared by persons who are messengers of hope is that of maintaining a healthy perspective in the face of difficulties or struggles. The capacity to maintain this more positive perspective is especially helpful when things simply do not go according to plan. It is this characteristic that allows one to say in the face of disappointment, "Oh well, maybe it just wasn't meant to be." "God must have a better plan in mind." "One door closes and another one will open."

In August of 2003, I traveled six hours by car to Albuquerque, New Mexico in hopes of seeing the planet Mars through a high powered telescope at the Museum of Natural History. On August 27th Mars would be only 34,646,418 miles away, its closest proximity to planet Earth in 60,000 years. On the evening of the special viewing, I eagerly awaited the once in a lifetime opportunity that would allow me to see Mars as very few people have seen it. But then, quite suddenly the evening skies over northern New Mexico began to turn cloudy, dark and ominous. And then, out of nowhere, the rain began to pour. The voice of the announcer came over the public address system to advise all those with special tickets to see the red planet that they would have to return tomorrow. Unfortunately, because I had to return home the following day, I would have to miss the viewing altogether.

Initially, I was angry and disappointed to say the least, but upon returning home the next day something happened that would give me an entirely different perspective and allow me to learn a valuable and much needed lesson. You see, while I had to forego the experience of seeing Mars through the high powered telescope atop the observatory in the mountains of northern New Mexico, I was given the opportunity to see it in a whole new way from my front porch back home underneath the beautiful clear skies of West Texas. As I stood gazing heavenward I noticed that it was easily the most brilliant star in all the sky, shining in the east and sparkling like the Hope Diamond. After a few weeks of admiring it every nightfall it soon occurred to me that not getting to see it at the observatory as I had originally hoped made it possible for me to appreciate it in ways I never would have, otherwise. And so, for weeks until it began to fade in the later stages of fall, it hovered every night over my front porch and taught me a valuable lesson. This is an example of what I mean by cultivating and maintaining a healthy perspective. It is living with the knowledge that often disappointments, failures, rejections, and sorrows can unintentionally bring about a greater good in our lives and in the lives of people around us. The more that we are able to maintain this perspective, the greater the possibility exists that we will be messengers of hope.

HOPE DOES NOT DISAPPOINT

In his seminal study, *Emotional Intelligence*, Daniel Goleman describes the value and meaning of living with hope:

> People with high levels of hope share certain traits, among them being able to motivate themselves, feeling resourceful enough to find ways to accomplish their objectives, reassuring themselves when in a tight spot that things will get better, being flexible enough to find different ways to get to their goals or to switch goals if one becomes impossible, and having the sense to break down a formidable task into smaller, manageable pieces. From the perspective of emotional intelligence, having hope means that one will not give in to overwhelming anxiety, a defeatist attitude or depression in the face of difficult challenges or setbacks. Indeed, people who are hopeful evidence less depression than others as they maneuver through life in pursuit of their goals, are less anxious in general and have fewer emotional distresses.[65]

If Goleman's assertion is true, and I believe that it is, it simply underscores a truth spoken long ago in the Scriptures by Paul the Apostle. Addressing a community of believers who underwent great trials and persecutions for their acceptance of the Christian message, Paul's words have been handed down from generation to generation in order to give people hope in their times of trial: "…We boast of the hope we have of sharing God's glory! We also boast of our troubles, because we know that trouble produces endurance, endurance brings God's approval, and his approval creates hope. This hope does not disappoint us, for God has poured out his love into our hearts by means of the Holy Spirit, who is God's gift to us."[66]

Similarly, the Hebrew prophet, Isaiah exhorts the people of Israel to put their hope in God, lest they give in to discouragement or despair: "Don't you know? Haven't you heard? The Lord is the everlasting God; he created all the world. He never grows tired or weary. No one understands his thoughts. He strengthens those who are weak and tired. Even those who are young grow weak; young people can fall exhausted. But those who trust in the Lord for help will find their strength renewed. They will rise on wings like eagles; they will run and not get weary; they will walk and not grow weak."[67]

DAMIEN THE LEPER

One who put his hope in God in order that he might become a messenger of hope to the hopeless was Damien de Veuster. In a moving account of his life, Margaret Bunson details his sixteen years spent caring for the lepers on the Island of Molokai, Hawaii.

The building projects he started upon his arrival would continue throughout his lifetime. When Kalaupapa was opened for Hansen's disease patients, Damien repaired the landing-place road and started a new community of new small whitewashed houses there. He worked as late as 1888 on the houses, even though the disease had crippled him and had started to drain away his remarkable strength. By doing the work himself, Damien set an example and offered the patients the first glimmers of hope. They soon joined and the houses began to spring up everywhere…He visited every patient at least once a week. When he first arrived, he discovered living 'corpses' lying abandoned in clumps of grass along the back trails. These victims had been dumped there by fellow lepers or had crawled there to die alone…Damien went to the hospital every morning gathering up the drugs, bandages, oils and other materials sent to the settlement…and then he started his rounds…He disinfected the sores that appeared on their bodies, bandaged the stumps or damaged limbs, cut away rotting flesh, and even amputated certain parts of their bodies that were in the last stages of putrefaction. This was not done with grace and calm. From the start Damien admitted freely that in the first weeks he had to leave the sides of the patients again and again, staggering outside to retch and lose the contents of his stomach. At other times he suffered blinding headaches because of the stench coupled with the nervous tension that developed as a result of his close contact with the lepers in his act of ministering to them.[68]

While all of us would agree that the actions of Damien de Veuster on behalf of the lepers of Molokai took extraordinary courage and faith, those who have researched his life agree that the beginning of his time in Molokai was anything but heroic. One account of his arrival on the island speaks of the transformative power of God that gave the 33 year old Belgian missionary the strength to carry on when all seemed lost. When Damien arrived by steamer he was warned by the ship's captain that before long he would give up and return to the ship as had all the other clergymen before him.

As the priest prepared to step from the large ship to a small rowboat waiting to take him ashore, the leper at the oars held out his hand to help the priest into the boat. Seized by the fear of leprosy, the priest refused the man's hand. Hurt and separation showed in the leper's eyes as he held out the oar for the priest to grasp. Arriving at the colony, Father Damien found his church building in shambles and his congregation nonexistent. The lepers wanted nothing to do with him and his touch-me-not brand of Christianity. The priest beat on the bell to summon people to the church, but the lepers turned deaf ears to all his pleas and calls. Beaten and giving up, Father Damien made his way back to the ship, which had returned to the colony. On board, something happened that changed his life and literally transformed the leper colony. A load of lumber intended for another Catholic parish was on board. Seeing it, the priest demanded that the captain drop the lumber off here for the lepers. The captain refused. Also on board was a fresh band of untouchable lepers to be dropped at the colony. Father Damien, caught up in a cause greater than himself, forgot about his fear and, in love, picked up a little girl who had leprosy. Holding her close he gently kissed her little check. Then he threatened the captain that unless he lowered the lumber and left it for the leper colony, the little girl would kiss him. The fearful captain immediately agreed to the priest's demand. Word quickly spread that the priest had touched the little girl with leprosy. By the time Father Damien arrived back at the colony with the load of lumber and the new band of lepers, the colony's citizens had gathered excitedly to see what was happening. Father Damian announced that instead of using the lumber to build the church first, they would together build a hospital to care for the needs of the people...As Father Damien reached out and touched the untouchable; love came alive, and worked the miracle. Estranged, suffering, lonely people drew together in serving, caring, healing love for one another.[69]

The story of Damien de Veuster reminds us that hope enables the weary and despairing to look beyond the present moment to a brighter day to come. Even when things look absolutely hopeless, if we persevere like Damien, inevitably God will turn our *mourning into morning.* And an unexpected light will penetrate through the thickest fog and gloom and dispel the darkness of the night so that we can find our way home to the harbor of peace and tranquility.

GO AND REPAIR MY HOUSE WHICH YOU SEE IS FALLING DOWN

In time, Damien saw in the face of the lepers of Molokai, the face of hope and the human face of God. In a strikingly similar way another young man who lived in the early part of the 12th century also gained a reputation among the people of Italy for his care and love for lepers. The young man, Francesco Di Pietro Bernardone, was born the son of a wealthy cloth merchant and grew up to help his father run the family business. Near the turn of the century a terrible war broke out between Francesco's home town of Assisi and the city of Perugia. Francesco, by then a young soldier, was taken prisoner of war and remained in captivity for over a year. After being released he knelt down to pray before a crucifix in the village church of San Damiano when he heard a voice saying. "Go and repair my house which you see is falling down." Francesco took the sound of this voice as a sign from God which led him to renounce his family's wealth and all of his material belongings.

During the next three years of his life he rebuilt the church of San Damiano by begging for money from the people of the town of Assisi. All during this time he continued to live a life of poverty, identifying himself with the most destitute and penniless of society. Afterwards, he gathered a group of seven middle aged men around him and they established a hermitage near the outskirts of Assisi. The hermitage, Portiuncula, was situated near an already established leper colony, and consisted of a modest chapel and huts where the brothers slept on the floor. For the next twenty years of his life, he would dedicate his life to preaching to and serving the poorest of the poor. In 1226, at the age of 45, he would die from a lack of medical attention, but by then his band of brothers had grown to number 5,000 strong.

Francesco, like Damien after him, became the face of hope for the lepers and the most despised members of society. In a prayer composed by Francesco, he exhorts his brothers to bring hope where there is despair and light where there is darkness. It is truly a prayer for all times and for all people. May all who pray it, like Francesco; become the face of hope for others. And, may it be a constant reminder that even in the throes of darkness and despair, God can surely turn our mourning into morning.

PRAYER OF SAINT FRANCIS OF ASSISI

Lord, make me an instrument
Of Your peace
Where there is hatred, let me sow love.
Where there is injury, pardon,
Where there is doubt, faith.
Where there is despair, hope,
Where there is darkness, light,
and where there is sadness, joy.
O Divine Master, grant that
I may not so much seek to be
consoled, as to console;
To be understood, as to understand;
To be loved, as to love;
For it is in giving that we receive—
It is in pardoning that
We are pardoned;
And it is in dying that
We are born to eternal life.

THE BEAUTIFUL FACE OF THE ELEPHANT MAN

In the early 1980's a movie set in Victorian England depicted the life of the elephant man. Shot in black and white, the film conveys in eerie tones the pain of a man who must conceal his face because it is so grotesque and disfigured. His disfigurement is so shocking to onlookers, he is exploited by a carnival side show as a freak, so that paying customers can gawk at his ugliness while shouting obscenities to mock him. It is only when the elephant man is discovered by a prominent doctor, who treats his wounds and cares for him, that he is able to reveal his inner identity. Once he is surrounded by people who care for him and are willing to look beyond his physical appearance, he begins to reveal his true identity as one capable of quoting Shakespeare and the Bible. In time, others begin to see that he is a deeply kind and spiritual person.

Damien de Veuster and Francis of Assisi were willing to look beyond the physical characteristics of the lepers, which in turn bestowed upon those they encountered the freedom to reveal their true inner beauty. When we are willing to do the same for others they will see in us, as they saw in Damien and Francis, the human face of hope. Then God will transform their darkness into light and their despair into hope, and we will be able to look upon the face of the elephant man with love.

Chapter VII

The Bridge Builder Has a Face

How we behave toward each other and toward the world does determine what will happen to us. With technology and weaponry, with the means to profoundly affect the environment, we as human beings carry the fate of this world in our hands. What is true of humanity on a large scale is true of each human being on a small scale. We are each part of the great task of tikkun olam ("repairing the world"), parents and children alike. God has made an interdependent world. All creatures are connected. We are partners, parents and children alike, all of us tied together and tied to God; what we do touches everyone.[70]

LOVE YOUR ENEMY AND BUILD HIM A BRIDGE

In the movie classic, *The Bridge Over the River Kwai*, a group of British soldiers held in a Japanese P.O.W. camp during World War II are put in the unenviable position of building a bridge for their enemies. As the movie unfolds the Japanese colonel in charge of the prison camp insists that the British soldiers, including their officers, must build a bridge over the River Kwai to enable the Japanese to move supplies. The British commander refuses to allow his officers to do forced labor. After a confrontation of wills where the Japanese try to break the spirit of the British, the Japanese finally give in to the demands of their prisoners in order for the bridge to be built on time. In the end, the British, motivated by a code of honor and discipline, construct a bridge for their enemies.

In real life, as in the movies, sometimes we too must be willing to build bridges for our enemies. Jesus teaches his disciples this lesson when he says, "You have heard that it was said, 'Love your friends, hate your enemies.' But now I tell you: love your enemies and pray for those who persecute you, so that you may become the children of your Father in heaven. For he makes his sun to shine on bad people and good people alike, and gives rain to those who do good and to those who do evil."[71]

Jesus' instruction on the love of enemies is not simply a matter of words. He often puts this difficult ideal into practice in his own life. His utterance from the cross, "Forgive them, Father! They don't know what they are doing," is but one example.[72] Another is his healing of the servant of the Roman soldier. In the world view of many of his contemporaries, it was necessary to maintain a distance and separation from the Romans who occupied their homeland. But in this particular instance, Jesus gives healing to the servant of the enemy of his people. In order to appreciate how radical a departure from the norm this must have seemed, an incident from John's gospel will illustrate. When Jesus is brought before Pilate the Jews are forbidden to enter the Praetorium for fear that they will be defiled, and thus, be forbidden to participate in the Passover meal. Similarly, this is not the only example given by a New Testament writer where contact with a Gentile renders a Jew unclean. The author of the Acts of the Apostles tells of Peter's entrance into the home of Cornelius, a Gentile. Peter said, "You yourselves know very well that a Jew is not allowed by his religion to visit or associate with Gentiles. But God has shown me that I must not consider any person ritually unclean or defiled."[73] It can be said about Jesus that not only did he spend his life and ministry building bridges for his enemies, and taught his disciples to do the same, but also, he built bridges for his friends and followers. Countless times during the course of his life he built bridges of kindness, forgiveness, hope, and compassion.

THE FIRST GRADE TEACHER WHO BUILT A BRIDGE

Jesus invites us to be builders of bridges for others in our own lives. One of my favorite examples of one who built bridges for me in my life was my first grade teacher, Edith Waits. "Mrs. Waits," as I first came to know her, was a bridge builder for me from the time I was six years old. She taught first grade in our little neighborhood school a short distance from our family home. Having taught my older brother and sister before me, she knew me, or at least knew about me, long before my first day of school. She once visited our home, along with all the other homes of all her students. To this day I'm not sure how she communicated with my mother, who spoke only a few words of English. Nevertheless, they got along very well, with my mother speaking Spanish and Mrs. Waits speaking English. As my sixth birthday approached, Mrs. Waits asked my mother to bake me a birthday cake and bring it to school. She said all my classmates could have a piece of cake. The cake my mother baked was decorated with six candles and a little plastic cowboy on a horse. After the cake was all gone I announced to Mrs. Waits, "I want you to have this cowboy!" and she gladly took it.

Twenty years after that birthday, and long after Mrs. Waits had retired from teaching, I was ordained a priest. During the ordination ceremony, seated in the Cathedral church not far from my family and friends, was Mrs. Waits. Unbeknownst to me, my sister Helen had invited her to attend. Although she had been a very devoted Baptist all her life, and had never attended Catholic Mass, much less an ordination ceremony, she later told me that she wouldn't have missed it for the world. Afterwards, while greeting guests in a receiving line, I embraced Mrs. Waits and told her how happy I was to see her after so many years. As we spoke, she took from her purse a handkerchief and holding it out to me uncovered the little plastic cowboy that had been on my birthday cake so long ago. She said, "Do you remember giving me this on your birthday? I kept it for you all these years and now I want you to have it back to remind you how special you are to me." Mrs. Waits built for me a bridge of kindness. Long after I was no longer her student she continued to care for me and pray for me. And her example has often inspired me to do likewise for others entrusted to my care.

THE OLD MAN AND THE BRIDGE

The following poem has inspired countless people to become bridge builders for others:

An old man, going a lone highway,
Came, at the evening, cold and gray,
To a chasm, vast and deep, and wide,
Through which was flowing a sullen tide.
The old man crossed in the twilight dim;
The sullen stream had no fears for him;
But he turned, when safe on the other side,
And built a bridge to span the tide.
"Old man," said a fellow pilgrim, near,
"You are wasting strength with building here;
Your journey will end with the ending day;
You never again must pass this way;
You have crossed the chasm, deep and wide
Why build you the bridge at the eventide"
The builder lifted his old gray head:
"Good friend, in the path I have come," he said,
"There followeth after me today
A youth, whose feet must pass this way,
This chasm, that has been naught to me,
To that fair-haired youth may a pitfall be.
He, too, must cross in the twilight dim;
Good friend, I am building the bridge for *him*."[74]

The old man is willing to make a sacrifice to build a bridge out of consideration for the young man who will later follow in his footsteps. He does so in order that the young man may avoid some of the pitfalls and dangers that lay before him. He has already crossed to the other side, so his motivation for building the bridge is none other than love and concern for the one to come after him.

Some years ago, two modern day troubadours hit upon a similar theme when they captivated a whole generation of listeners by singing about a bridge over troubled waters. In their lyrics Simon and Garfunkel described the same kind of altruism when they sang about the friend who lays down his or her life over stormy waters like a bridge.

A King Kneels Before His Subjects

Jesus, the bridge builder, teaches us in the Gospels that he is always willing to lay down his life for us. When times get difficult and friends are nowhere to be found, he reminds us that he is willing to dry the tears from our eyes and to be a bridge for us. In his farewell discourse to his friends Jesus spoke about laying down one's life for his friends when he said, "My commandment is this: love one another, just as I love you. The greatest love you can have for your friends is to give your life for them."[75] Prior to this, he also spoke to them about following his example of unselfishness when he washed the feet of the disciples during the Passover meal. Following this radical gesture, preserved in the gospel of John, he said, "I have set an example for you, so that you will do just what I have done for you."[76]

Over the centuries Christian writers have struggled to put into words the self-sacrificing nature of Jesus washing his disciples' feet. Words like humility, mercy, love, compassion, gentleness, tenderness, and self-giving have been used by writers to describe this act of pure love. C. Gene Wilkes captures how radical this gesture of Jesus truly was when it came to laying down his own life for a friend who would betray him.

Jesus washing Judas's feet still baffles me. My natural tendencies would say, "If you knew the guy was a traitor, why didn't you get rid of him?" Others would judge, "If you were a good leader, Jesus, you would have known what was going on and stopped it from happening." ...The picture is amazing. Here was the King of kings kneeling before the one who had already sold him to the enemy for thirty pieces of silver. They both knew the deal was done. Both knew the end result. Still Jesus did not skip Judas when it came his turn to be washed. Judas had a need -as all the others did. He, too, must see his Savior kneeling at his feet before he saw him hanging on a cross. Only love beyond human capacity can motivate a leader to humble himself before a person who may be turning him over to his enemies.[77]

From our reading of the account of the washing of the disciple's feet, one important dimension of the Christian life comes clearly into focus. Each of us who seeks to be his follower in the modern world is called upon by Jesus to be a builder of bridges. Like the bridge over troubled water, like the old man who crossed the chasm vast and deep, like Edith Waits, we too are invited to build bridges of kindness, courage, hope, and compassion for others along life's highway. Sometimes we will build those bridges for our friends and families, other times we will be invited by God to build bridges for our enemies and those who would betray us. And each of us, no matter how young or old, no matter the color of our skin, no matter the material resources at our disposal, has the God-given potential to be a builder of bridges. When we are willing to put at God's disposal our hands, our hearts, our perspiration, and our lives, no matter how limited or broken our lives may seem, then God will provide the bricks and mortar, the "stuff" from which bridges are made.

Often, however, we are told by others around us that we do not have or possess the "stuff" we need to build bridges, and, therefore, our efforts will seem to have little or no impact. Sometimes in childhood, and well into adulthood, we are exposed to a steady chorus of comments like, "You'll never amount to much." "You'll only make matters worse." "You're not good enough." "Let someone else try." These and other statements like them can wound and, worse still, can limit our belief in ourselves to be bridge builders as Jesus invites us to be. Over time, such negative feedback begins to erode our self-esteem, self-love, and self-confidence. And in the face of such pessimism and negativity we will begin to hear an inner voice that says, "I'm not good enough." "I'm not holy enough." "I'm not worthy enough." "I'm not strong enough." "I'm not important enough." It is in the face of such inner self-doubt and pessimism that Jesus wants to speak to us with the sound of another voice. It is a voice that speaks tenderly, "You are good." "You are worthy." "You are strong." "And if you lend me your hands, feet, voice, and heart, I will make you a builder of bridges."

Lest we live under the mistaken illusion that God only chooses the powerful, the wealthy, the beautiful, or the influential to build bridges for him, we have only to look to the Bible to see that this is not usually the case. In Moses he chose a castaway who was later guilty of murdering an Egyptian for striking a Hebrew slave. Yet, God appointed him to be the great liberator of his people. In David he chose a young shepherd boy who later committed adultery with a woman whose husband he then arranged to be killed in battle. Yet, God anointed him King of Israel where he reigned for forty years. In Paul he chose an enemy and persecutor of the earliest Jewish converts to Christianity. Yet, God empowered him to be a great missionary and bearer of the good news of Jesus' death and resurrection to the Gentiles.

HE TOLD ME EVERYTHING I HAVE DONE

One poignant example of Jesus empowering the seemingly unworthy and unlovable to be his bridge builder is found in chapter four of John's gospel. In this beautiful episode described in compelling terms by John, a woman approached Jesus at a public well. A conversation ensued between Jesus and the woman when he asked her for a drink of water. Initially the woman was reluctant to talk to him because of the prohibitions that existed at the time surrounding contact between Samaritans and Jews. Nevertheless, Jesus befriended the woman and treated her with dignity and compassion. Afterwards, the woman began to tell her story about her encounter with Jesus to the people of the town. Later on it is revealed that because of the woman's testimony other Samaritans came to believe that Jesus was the messiah. It made no difference to Jesus that the woman already had five husbands and the man she was living with was not her husband. Nevertheless, he still invited her to be a builder of bridges for others. John put it this way, "Many of the Samaritans in that town believed in Jesus because the woman had said, 'He told me everything I have ever done.' So when the Samaritans came to him, they begged him to stay with them, and Jesus stayed there two days. Many more believed because of his message, and they told the woman, 'We believe now, not because of what you said, but because we ourselves have heard him, and we know that he really is the Savior of the world.'"[78]

This particular encounter between Jesus and the woman at the well is striking for a number of reasons. For me, it underscores in bold terms Jesus' own willingness to put into practice his teaching that the law of loving one's neighbor and extending mercy to one's enemy far supercedes any other law including the laws that preserve ritual and bodily purity. In touching the life and heart of the woman at the well, Jesus rejects the law that prohibits contact with those thought to be impure. He builds a bridge of compassion to the woman, so that she in turn can become a bridge for others.

Donald Senior in his book, *Jesus: A Gospel Portrait*, captures this characteristic of Jesus' way of loving others as the most important of God's commandments.

> Jesus would observe the Sabbath regulations–but not when they formed a barrier to the demands of love and compassion…Certain foods were to be avoided. Numerous rituals were performed daily…Contact with gentiles and those ignorant of the law were

not permitted. Jesus' response again cuts against the very grain of this approach...One's own integrity, the active response of love and compassion, defines true purity in the eyes of God rather than attempts to maintain external purity...For Jesus every response, every decision, every action had to proceed from love. This defined the meaning of integrity. Jesus' insistence on love and compassion and his revulsion at legalism and hypocrisy ultimately find their authority in his intimate relationship with God...It was God's love that was showered on the good and the bad, that wrote off the debt, that searched out the lost, that rejoiced in repentance, that demanded attention to the weightier laws of justice, mercy, and compassion. Jesus' experience of the love of this God, his Abba, is the source of his teaching.[79]

In essence Jesus does not erect barriers between himself and sinners. Instead, he shatters the walls between himself and others like a thousand Berlin Walls tumbling down.

What the World Disdains, God Ordains

Another classic example of one used by God to be a builder of bridges, in spite of his human weakness and personal brokenness, is John Newton. John Newton is best known for penning the beautiful lyrics to the song, "Amazing Grace." Many generations of Christians have come to know the lyrics by heart:

Amazing grace! How sweet the sound.
That saved a wretch like me.
I once was lost, but now I'm found. Was blind but now I see.
T'was grace that taught my heart to fear, and grace my fears relieved.
How precious did that grace appear the hour I first believed.

From the time John Newton was a little boy until his mother's death when he was only seven years old, she taught him Christian values. At the age of eleven, John's father took him to sea where they captured and traded African slaves. In his biography of Newton, Steve Turner summarized the popular version of events that led Newton from captain of a slave ship to Christian convert and finally teacher and preacher. "He was a slave captain whose ship was hit by a severe storm. Terrified by the prospect of death he vowed to abandon the trade if his life was spared. He avoided death, and true to his word set his cargo of slaves free, left the trade, and devoted his life to writing songs. His best known song, "Amazing Grace," is about his rejection of the slave trade and how his eyes have been opened to its evil."[80]

In the later years of his life Newton became an ordained minister in the Church of England and pastor of the small village church of Olney, England. He began to preach the Word of God to the townspeople of Olney in his old sailor's coat, using his own life as an example of the journey from debauchery and blasphemy to soul searching and finally conversion to Christianity. While according to Turner, "The changes in his outlook and behavior came slowly and painfully," there is no denying that the former slave trader became an inspiration to others and a bridge builder for God.[81] The story of John Newton also serves to remind us that God often uses unexpected means or unconventional people to be his channels of grace. Who would ever imagine that someone like John Newton could undergo a conversion that would result in his writing the beautiful words of "Amazing Grace?" Who would ever imagine that a slave trader, the son of a slave ship captain, would become an inspiration to others and would ultimately inspire others to fight for the abolishment of slavery in England? In the case of John Newton, what the world disdained, God ordained. The stories of John Newton, the woman at the well, Moses, King David, and Paul are ultimately intended to teach us that each of us, despite our human limitations, despite our fears and unworthiness, is called upon by God to be a builder of bridges for others. Jesus did not come to invite only a select group of people to be among his bridge builders. Instead, his invitation to be a builder of bridges goes out to all people.

JESUS, THE JEWISH LAYMAN

In the ancient world the title of bridge builder, or "pontifex" from the Latin (*pontis* meaning bridge and *facere* meaning to make) was originally a designation reserved for the emperor in Rome. In the late fourth century the title of pontifex became a title of honor accorded the bishop of Rome stressing his ministry of "bridging the gap" between heaven and earth, the divine and the human.

Historically, the use of pontifex was reserved for those who by their office held the title or office of bishop or emperor of Rome. Thus, it would seem that in the ancient world view, only those who held such offices could possess the power to "bridge the gap" between heaven and earth. But in reading the accounts of the gospels and searching for a more meaningful understanding of the life and person of Jesus, it seems that Jesus does not endow the power to bridge the gap between heaven and earth to only a select few who hold special titles and offices. In fact, this is all the more true when we consider the indisputable evidence that Jesus himself did not hold, possess, nor did he accept the title of priest. Indeed, Jesus, the bridge builder, was never a member of the clergy or priesthood of his day. In his time there were rabbis, priests, high priests, Pharisees, Levites, and scribes. According to the gospels, Jesus was a rabbi not a priest. This meant that in his time he would have been seen by all as a member of the Jewish laity and not as one who belonged to a priestly class.

The fact that he was a layman, and not a member of any clerical class, has something very important to teach us about the life and person of Jesus of Nazareth. In the first instance he was able to bring about the kingdom of God precisely because he was free of the strictures and restrictions of the temple priesthood of his day. Unencumbered by the legal and juridical requirements of the temple institution he was free to heal, forgive, and ultimately restore sinners and outsiders to the mercy and grace of God. More important to Jesus than preserving and observing the ritual requirements of purity, was his desire to "bridge the gap" between heaven and earth for those who lived in sorrow, fear, and shame. The preservation of a system based on temple rituals was important to the temple priests, while doing the work of mercy and justice was more important to Jesus, the Jewish layman.

While the temple priests exercised their priesthood by performing the rituals that ensured and preserved cultic purity, Jesus simply went about building bridges for others. Indeed, he challenged those who were mere temple functionaries to move beyond the observance of cultic rituals, where they emphasized ritual offerings, to a life of mercy that de-emphasized the cultic/ritual aspects of the faith. Instead of a life centered on ritual offering, Jesus invites them, and us, to a life centered on acceptance of others, mercy, healing, and compassion.

Perhaps a scene in the Gospels will bring this point more clearly into focus. While eating at the home of Matthew, the tax collector, Jesus is joined at the table by tax collectors and sinners. When questioned by the Pharisees about his dinner companions he responds, "People who are well do not need a doctor, but only those who are sick. Go and find out what is meant by the scripture that says: 'It is kindness that I want, not animal sacrifices.' I have not come to call respectable people, but outcasts."[82]

To further illustrate this important aspect in the life of Jesus of Nazareth, and what this dimension of his life has to teach us about our shared responsibility to bridge the gap between heaven and earth, I believe the writings of John Meier can be especially helpful in presenting a more authentic portrayal of the earthly Jesus.

One aspect of Jesus' family background was so obvious to his Jewish contemporaries that, as far as we know, neither he nor they ever commented on it during his lifetime. Yet this aspect has been so overlooked or misunderstood by later Christians that it needs to be emphasized. It is the simple fact that Jesus was born a Jewish layman. There is no reliable historical tradition that he was of Leviticus or priestly descent.[83]

According to Meier, the title of "high priest" ascribed to Jesus by the author of the Letter to the Hebrews is a *spiritual* not a *temporal* designation. In the eyes of the author, Jesus is the great "high priest" by virtue of his atoning sacrifice on the cross and his exaltation to heaven after his death. Thus, Jesus becomes our great high priest only by undergoing a sacrificial death on Calvary in order to atone for the sins of all humanity. Furthermore, adds Meier, "Thus, for all the theology of Christ the high priest in Hebrews, the epistle in no way contradicts the Gospel presentation of Jesus as a Jewish layman. Therefore, even for the Epistle to the Hebrews, while Jesus was on earth, he was a Jewish layman, not a priest."[84]

I am spending a considerable amount of time on this point in order to underscore a very important lesson in all of this. That is, each of us, whether we are a layperson, priest, rabbi, minister, or preacher is called upon by God to bridge the gap between heaven and earth. Ultimately, to be a bridge builder does not require that one have a special title or that one be an ordained member of the clergy. As we can see from the New Testament, not even Jesus possessed a special title or privileged status. The clear lack of such a title or office, nevertheless, did not diminish his capacity to bring hope to the hopeless, healing to the broken-hearted and mercy to those often shunned by the religious authorities of his day. And, to the degree that we are willing to build bridges of kindness, compassion, forgiveness, courage, and hope for others as Jesus did, will we be able to be a "pontifex," able to bridge the gap between heaven and earth, the divine and the human.

SHE BUILT A BRIDGE IN THE DESERT OF IRAQ

One who became a "pontifex" for the people of the war torn country of Iraq was Fern Holland. Raised by a single mother in Miami, Oklahoma, Fern graduated from high school as homecoming queen and salutatorian of her class. After earning a law degree from the University of Tulsa, Fern went to work for the law firm of Conner and Winters in the field of environmental law. But after four years of practicing law and winning a number of cases, Fern made a decision that would alter the course of her life. She announced to her law firm that she was joining the Peace Corp and would soon be leaving for Africa. During the next three years Fern lived and worked with the poorest of the poor in Namibia and Guinea. In both instances she championed the rights of women, especially women who were victims of physical and sexual abuse. During this time in her life one colleague said of Fern, "[she] was making a difference in young girls' lives. She was helping to prevent rapes and torture…but always through the law."[85]

In 2003 she accepted the invitation of Paul Bremer, the United States Provisional Administrator of Iraq, to move to that war torn country. Noted for her work on human rights issues, Fern was given the task of helping to initiate 18 centers for democracy, women and human rights. Based in south central Iraq, Fern went to work with a passion. Before long she began to gain notoriety among the local citizens who saw her as a brave and courageous young woman working on their behalf. By December of 2003 Fern had become a key player in helping the Iraqis draft the section of their new constitution pertaining to the rights of women.

But by the spring of 2004 the social and political climate in Iraq began to take an even more ominous turn. In an e-mail addressed to one of her former law partners, Fern captured how difficult and unpredictable the situation had become.

Two little old women from a nearby village came to see me today…They are widows. They wear all black. All you can see is their faces-no hair or neck. They don't wear gloves and you can see their hands…dry and cracked and evidence of broken fingers from years ago, and huge knuckles from years of manual labor. Their faces wrinkled and dark, no makeup but two small faded blue circles on their chins-tattoos. One of Saddam's thugs grew crops on their land, and they thought they could remove him upon liberation…No such luck. He built a house on their land and refused to leave. They have court orders and everything and nobody will move the guy. Everyone's afraid of him…I'm going to see him Saturday morning, along with the little ladies, the manager of the new women's center, the judge and a couple of Iraqi policemen.[86]

Later, some of her friends in Iraq would say that Fern even arranged to have a bulldozer smash the man's house. This e-mail to her colleague back in the United States gives us a feel for just how committed and brave a person Fern Holland really was. When asked by a friend while on a visit home why she was putting herself in such great peril, Fern responded, "I love the Iraqi people. They are so sweet and kind and open and appreciative, and we can really make a difference there. I have no choice but to return."[87]

Less than a week after sending the e-mail about the plight of the Iraqi women, Fern, along with two of her coworkers, was ambushed and shot to death with an AK- 47 as she traveled the road from Karbala to Hilla. While her body was transported back to her native Oklahoma for burial, Fern's spirit and presence continue to pervade the Iraqi countryside and more importantly, the Iraqi people she had grown to love. In another e-mail she sent to a friend in the United States prior to her death she wrote, "I love the work, and if I die, know that I'm doing precisely what I want to be doing-working to organize and educate human rights activists and women's groups-human rights and democracy education for independents who are motivated and capable of leading this country... We're doing all we can with the brief time we've got left. It's a terrible race. Wish us luck. Wish the Iraqis luck."[88]

I suspect most of us can point to at least one person in our lives who, like Fern Holland, has been a bridge builder for us, who has been the human face of God for us. Most of the time they have bridged the gap between heaven and earth for us by doing acts of loving kindness, compassion, mercy, and forgiveness on our behalf. Sometimes the bridge builders in our lives have been parents, children, spouses, neighbors, mentors, caregivers, and friends. At times they have been people who themselves bore the wounds of rejection and human brokenness. But whoever they are and regardless of how they have touched and impacted our lives, always they reveal to us God's face in human form. God says to us, through them, "Look at my face. Look at my face and know that it is the face of love."

GODS AND GENERALS AND THE FACE OF A LITTLE CHILD

In the epic drama, *Gods and Generals*, the character of Confederate General, Stonewall Jackson is portrayed in the movie as a brave and noble person forced into the terrible and tragic situation of leading men into battle during the American Civil War. In the midst of the terrible loss of life on the battlefield, the awful conditions of winter and the loneliness experienced from not having seen his wife and newborn child, General Jackson receives an unexpected gift. The gift is the warm embrace of a little child whose father is away at war. At the moment he receives the embrace, the gloom and sadness of war all around him is dispelled and at once the light of hope and the promise of a brighter day surround him and transform him. In the face of the little child he sees the face of his own child whom he cannot see and hold. It is the little child's face that restores him and makes him whole again. In the face of the little child he sees the human face of God.

Two thousand years ago in a remote and unassuming region of the world some lowly shepherds wondered if a little child born to humble parents could be the human face of God. After all, could the God who made the stars, the seas, and all living things, allow part of Himself to be born in such poverty and squalor? Imagine allowing someone you loved to be born among the cows, sheep and goats. We would never think of it. And yet, God allowed it. He allowed a part of Himself to be born completely human and helpless. After all, how powerful is a little baby? No one could argue that a little baby is completely vulnerable, dependent, and weak.

By allowing Himself to be born in a state of such weakness God is certainly teaching us something about Himself and us. I believe that He is saying, "In the person of my son I will weep when you are weeping. I will feel sorrow when you are rejected. My heart will feel your disappointment, your fears, your loneliness, your dreams, your happiness, your hopes, and your joys. "Look at me!" I who made the heavens, stars, planets, mountains, seas, and every living thing. Look at me, lying in a manger, where animals eat their food. Just look at my face! "Look at my face and know how much I love you. I will always love you. And you will not have to walk in darkness, anymore."

Endnotes

[1] John 21:15-19.

[2] *Murdered in Central America*, by Donna W. Brett and Edward T. Brett, Orbis Books, 1988. p. 176.

[3] Luke 22:42.

[4] Luke 1:38.

[5] From quote by Hannah Whitall Smith, p. 253, in *Guide to Prayer for Ministers and Other Servants* copywight © 1983 by Rueben P. Job and Norman Shawchuck. Used by permission of Upper Room Books®, http://www.bookstore.upperroom.org, 1-800-972-0433.

[6] *Toa Te Ching*, Loa-tzu; China, c. 604-531 B.C.E...,

[7] *The Holy Longing*, by Ronald Rolheiser, Doubleday, 1999 p. 125.

[8] *Archetypal Priests Are Not Always Ordained Priests*, Fr. Richard Rohr. AMERICA, April 5, 1997.

[9] *A World of Stories*, William J. Bausch, Twenty-Third Publications, 1998.

[10] Luke 24:36-39.

[11] Luke 24:15-16.

[12] John 20:16.

[13] Matthew 25:41-43.

[14] Barclay, William. The Gospel of Matthew Volume 2. Philadelphia: Westminster Press, 1975. p.325-326.

[15] Ibid.

[16] Ibid.

[17] *Oxford Dictionary of Saints,* Oxford University Press, Oxford, England, Pub. 1997, p. 290.

[18] *Lord Give Me Someone,* Anonymous.

[19] Matthew 28:20.

[20] Reprinted with the permission of Simon & Schuster Adult Publishing Group from *The Road Less Traveled and Beyond* by M. Scott Peck, M.D., copyright© 1997 by M. Scott Peck.

[21] *The Pope in the Holy Land: The Overview,* by Alessandra Stanley, New York Times, March 24, 2000.

[22] Ibid.

[23] Isaiah 61:1-3.

[24] Luke 10:26-38.

[25] *Hearing the Parables of Jesus.* Pheme Perkins, Paulist Press, 1981. p. 115.

[26] John 15:12.

[27] Oklahoma City National Memorial Inscription statement provided Courtesy of Oklahoma City National Memorial.

[28] Cornelius by Bob Green, Chicago Tribune (December 20, '99), ©1999 by Tribune Media Services, 435 N. Michigan Ave., Chicago, IL. 60611.

[29] Wolpe, David J. *Teaching Your Children About God.* Henry Holt and Company, Inc. 1993, p.186.

[30] *Let's Roll,* by Lisa Beamer, 2002, Tyndale House Publishers.

[31] *Father Mychal Judge,* by Michael Ford, 2002, Paulist Press, p.9-11.

[32] *The Confessions,* St. Augustine of Tagaste, c. 397-401 A.D.

[33] Luke 15: 7.

[34] Luke 7:48-50.

[35] Luke 5:30.

[36] Mark 2:15-16.

[37] Luke 6:37.

[38] Matthew 21:31.

[39] Luke 19:5-9.

[40] *The Historical Figure of Jesus,* by E.P. Sanders, (Allen Lane, 1993, Penguin Books, 1995). Copyright E.P. Sanders, 1993.

[41] Mark 14:9.

[42] Kushner, Harold S. *How Good Do Wo Have To Be?* Little Brown and Company, 1996, 43-44.

[43] Ibid.

[44] *The Spirituality of Imperfection* by Ernest Kurtz and Katherine Ketcham, 1992, Bantam Books; p. 29.

[45] Ibid.

[46] 1 John 4:10.

[47] Psalm 51.

[48] *A God of Incredible Surprises,* Virgilio Elizondo, Published by Rowman & Littlefield Publishers, Inc., 2003.

[49] Psalm 23.

[50] *Following Jesus, Biblical Reflections on Discipleship*, N.T. Wright, Published by William B. Eerdmans, Publishing Company, Grand Rapids, Michigan, 1994.

[51] Luke 1:30.

[52] Luke 2:10-11.

[53] Mark 4:39-40.

[54] Mark 6:50.

[55] Brown, Raymond E. "An Introduction to the New Testament." *The Anchor Bible Reference Library*. Ed. William Foxwell Albright and David Noel Freedman. New York: Doubleday, 1986. 133-134.

[56] *Churchill on Leadership*, Steven F. Hayward, Prima Publishing, 1997, p. 29.

[57] *Lincoln on Leadership*, Donald T. Phillips, 1992, Warner Books, New York, N.Y. p. 75.

[58] Barclay, William. *The Gospel of John, Volume 2, Revised Edition*. Philadelphia, PA: Westminster Press, 1975. 53-62.

[59] John 1:29.

[60] 23rd Psalm for Mothers, Unknown.

[61] *Dead Man Walking*, by Helen Prejean, C.S.J., Vintage Books, A Division of Random House, 1994, pp. 92-95.

[62] Ibid.

[63] *Creators Syndicate,* November 20, 1996 by Ann Landers.

[64] Excerpt from *The Gift of Peace*, by Cardinal Joseph Bernardin, (Loyola Press 1997). Reprinted with permission of Loyola Press. To order copies of this book, call 1-800-621-1008 or visit *www. loyolabooks.org.*

65 *Emotional Intelligence*, by Daniel Goleman, A Bantam Book, New York, New York, Published 1995.

66 Letter of Paul to the Romans, 5:2-5.

67 Isaiah 40:28-31.

68 *Father Damien, The Man and His Era*, by Margaret R. Bunson, Our Sunday Visitor Publishing Division, revised 1997, p.95-99.

69 *The Speaker Sourcebook*, by Glenn Van Ekeren, Prentice Hall Division of Simon and Schuster, New Jersey, Published 1988, p.250-251.

70 *Teaching Your Children About God*, Wolpe, David J., Henry Holt & Company, Inc., 1993, p. 140-141.

71 Matthew 5: 43-45.

72 Luke 23:34.

73 Acts 10:28.

74 *The Bridge Builder*, Dromgoole, Will Allen.

75 John 15: 12-13.

76 John 13:15.

77 *Jesus on Leadership*, C. Gene Wilkes, Tyndale House Publisher, 1998, p.166-167.

78 John 4:39-42.

79 *Jesus: A Gospel Portrait*, Paulist Press, by Donald Senior, C.P., pub. 1992 pp. 96-98.

80 *Amazing Grace*: The Story of America's Most Beloved Song, Steve Turner, Harper Collins Publishers, 2002.

81 Ibid.

82 Matthew 9:12-13.

83 *Marginal Jew: Rethinking the Historical Jesus*, John P. Meier, Anchor Bible Reference Library, Doubleday, 1991, p. 345-349.

84 Ibid.

85 "Fern Holland", *Dallas Morning News*, Granberry, Michael, April 19, 2004.

86 Ibid.

87 Ibid.

88 Ibid.

Appendix of Prayers

Trust

God of loving kindness, you who dwell in my heart, and know my every thought, grant me this day the grace to trust you for all that I need. May the indwelling of your grace help me to move beyond my daily doubts and fears and so place my trust in you.

When I am willing to open my heart, I see your face so clearly. It is a face of love and hope. Yet, at other times, my daily struggles cause my vision to be blurred and all seems dark before me. In those moments, speak to me, my God, and guide my steps toward the light.

Help me to see your face, and to trust that every breath I take is because you will it so. I believe that you, who made the heavens and the earth, also live and move and breathe in me. May I always be aware of your presence in the world. And, may I grow to trust you more each day, so that no obstacle, no struggle and no disappointment, can ever separate me from the love I feel for you and the love you have for me. AMEN

Mercy

Loving God, you who are the source of all goodness, be near me and calm my fears. In your infinite love, I pray that you will be merciful to me. Help me to move beyond my own self-interest. Help me to see beyond my own needs, in order that I may see *your face* in the poor, the stranger, the outcast, and the sinner.

Your mercy knows no bounds, your forgiveness has no limits, and yet, it is often I who judge. As you have been merciful to me, help me to be merciful to others. Help me to remember that as I judge others, I will be judged. As I forgive others, I will be forgiven. As I welcome others, I will be welcomed.

As I go throughout the course of my life, help me to remember that your own son was born in a stable, worked as a humble carpenter, and died between two criminals. May I take from his example the desire to live a humble life, thinking less of my own needs, and more of the needs of others. When I enter your heavenly kingdom, if it is your will for me to do so, do not judge me according to my sins, but rather in your goodness be merciful to me. AMEN

Compassion

Lord, you who healed the blind, embraced sinners, and cared for the sick, look upon me with compassion and love. When I feel unworthy of your love, it is then I need you the most. Teach me to trust that you are a compassionate and loving God.

Touch my life with your compassion for others. Help me to see others as you would see them. Help me to be gentle in my judgments. As I go about the tasks of daily life at work, school, church, and at home, I pray I may extend your compassionate touch to all. May every encounter of this day be a moment to encounter *You, as You* reveal your face in the least of your children.

And may every act of kindness given, remind me that it is *Jesus* I feed, serve, and love in the very least of my brothers and sisters. Lord, be compassionate to me in my hour of need. AMEN.

Forgiveness

Gentle and merciful God, I come before you this day as a sinner in need of your love. I believe you are full of compassion for those who come before you with a humble heart.

Often I wander far from you like the prodigal child wasting the gifts you have given me. I believe at those moments you will lead me home to you. As a loving parent embraces a lost child upon its safe return, as a shepherd binds the wounds of the lost sheep, I pray you will accept me with a loving embrace.

Give me a willingness to change my heart. Take away my selfishness and pride. As I gaze upon the face of your son on the cross, help me to forgive those who harm me with the same forgiveness I have received from you. May your son's saving death free me from the burden of sin and shame, and renew my heart, forever. AMEN

Courage

Lord God, you who breathed upon the waters and calmed the storms at sea, hear me and answer my plea. Often I grow weary as I go against the tide of worldly concerns and daily worries. Breathe upon me and calm my fears. Instill in me the grace to live out my convictions with courage.

When you ask me to do something difficult to bring about a greater good in my life and in the lives of others, I often feel afraid. It is then I must turn to you, my God. For it is in you that I find security and peace. With your courage to strengthen me I will never be alone.

Sustain me and I will not shrink from the challenges and difficulties of this day. Fill my heart with courage that I may be your *face* in this weary and wounded world. That in the midst of the storms that come I can hear your voice that speaks to me, "Courage! It is I. Do not be afraid." AMEN

Hope

God of eternal hope and infinite joy, be with me at the beginning of this new day.

In the midst of the sorrows and disappointments I may encounter, help me to be your light in the darkness.

Help me to resist falling into despair or depression. Instead, may I always be willing to give comfort to the afflicted, solace to mourners, encouragement to the sick, and support to the needy.

In my loneliness, doubts, and fears I need your hope to strengthen me. As I walk through the valleys of my life, may I gaze to the heavens and find hope in you. For in you my soul finds peace. In you my heart finds acceptance and joy.

And, as I come to the end of this day, may I sleep with the knowledge that tomorrow you will grant me the gift of new day. And when morning comes, you will refresh my soul and renew my hope in *You.* AMEN

Acknowledgements

I wish to express my thanks and appreciation to the following friends and colleagues who assisted me with the publication of this manuscript. God bless you, and the other wonderful people in my life, who have encouraged me and supported my efforts throughout the years.

For their suggestions and guidance in the area of content, I wish to thank: Virgilio Elizondo, Richard Rohr, Michael Jamail, Ron Rohlheiser, and Paul Bernier.

For their technical assistance and help with manuscript preparation, I wish to thank: Louise Cates, Dora Fierro, Eva Jimenez, Beverly Wink, Angie Pina, and Joe Lopez.

Affectionately,

The Author

About the Author

David R. Cruz is Pastor of Our Lady of Grace Catholic Church in Lubbock, Texas. He completed his theological studies and training for the priesthood at the Catholic University of Louvain in Belgium in 1986. Since then he has provided spiritual care for people in rural communities, hospitals, prisons, and shelters for victims of domestic violence. He is past President of Assumption Seminary in San Antonio, Texas.

Printed in the United States
137419LV00005B/2/A

9 781414 107110